Message to the Motorist:  and READ

Safe and responsible driving begins with you! Be a safe driver and drive defensively. By being a defensive driver you will have the knowledge, skills and right attitude for safe driving.

This study guide will teach you about road signs, traffic control signals, pavement markings, driving responsibly, and how to get and keep your driver's licence.

This study guide is one of many sources to give you the skills and knowledge you need for getting your learner's Class 7 and GDL probationary Class 5 licence. It also contains information to help towards your full-privilege Class 5 licence. It is also recommended that you consult other sources for more detailed and specific information, such as:

- Government of Alberta—Driver's Licence, www.servicealberta.gov.ab.ca/ Drivers_Licence.cfm

- Government of Alberta—Programs and Services, www.transportation. alberta.ca

- Government of Alberta—Drivers and Motor Vehicles, www.servicealberta. gov.ab.ca/Drivers_MotorVehicles.cfm

Note: Laws are constantly changing so obtain the most recent updates from the Alberta Traffic Safety Act.

It is also recommended that new drivers take an approved driver education course to gain positive habits and learn and perfect the skills needed for safe driving.

Education, practice, commitment to safety, observing the rules and advice in this study guide and other sources will help you get and stay on the road safely.

How to Use This Study Guide

Read everything carefully. The sample test questions numbered 1–200 and the road test section are designed to help you get your learner's (Class 7), probationary (Class 5-GDL) and full operator (Class 5) licence. **Please note: This study guide is for general reference only; consult other sources for more detailed information.**

Questions 1–102 are about traffic signs, such as regulatory, warning, and construction signs, to name a few. Traffic control signals and pavement markings are also included in this section.

Questions 103–200 are about responsible and safe driving, starting with what to do when you get in a car, to steering out of a skid, and more.

ⓘ For each question, select the most appropriate response, without looking below at the added information section. These information boxes sometimes give the answer away. Other times they will provide you with valuable added information to help with your understanding.

You will be asked some of these sample test questions on the actual knowledge test. **Please note: The actual test questions will vary. So, study this guide and make sure you know and understand all the information.**

Sample question

145. **Under what circumstances are cell phones not allo**
    a) When you use your cell phone to text.
    b) When you use your hand-held cell phone to chat
    c) When you use your cell phone to check and send
    d) All of the above.
  ⓘ Alberta's Distracted Driver legislation restricts drivers from us
    other restrictions.

Check your answers on the inside back cover to see how well you scored. *Could you pass?*

Questions on the Knowledge Test can include these topics:

✔ Regulatory signs

✔ Warning signs

✔ Permissive manoeuvre signs

✔ Prohibitive manoeuvre signs

✔ Road condition signs

✔ Traffic control signals

✔ Lane driving

✔ Using headlights

✔ Parking

✔ Speed limits

✔ Vehicle breakdown

✔ Entering and exiting a highway

✔ Passing vehicles

✔ Sharing the road

✔ Approaching an emergency vehicle or school bus

All sample test questions will help you understand the many things you need to know at all driving levels. Safe driving requires knowledge, skill gained through practice and a commitment to safety.

Once you have had your learner's licence for 12 months, and have practised for many hours with a fully licensed non-GDL probationary driver, you can book your first road test to get your stage two GDL probationary Class 5 licence. You will be evaluated on what you have learned from this study guide, in your driver education course and from other sources.

The road test section explains what to bring, what you are tested on, and what the examiner looks for during a road test. Your first road test will test general driving skills and knowledge. The advanced road test will evaluate you on more advanced driving skills. Read through this section of the study guide to help prepare for your test.

Sample illustration.

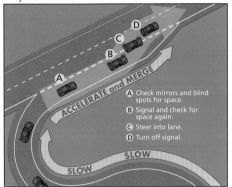

ACCELERATE and MERGE

Ⓐ Check mirrors and blind spots for space.
Ⓑ Signal and check for space again.
Ⓒ Steer into lane.
Ⓓ Turn off signal.

SLOW   SLOW

Alberta's Graduated Driver Licensing (GDL) Program

To drive in Alberta you must have a valid driver's licence and it must be the right one for the vehicle you want to drive. Vehicles include cars, trucks, motorcycles, buses, etc. (see the chart on page 7 for different vehicles and the type of licence required to drive each one).

Becoming a Fully Licensed Driver

Alberta has a Graduated Driver Licensing Program that requires all drivers to graduate from the first level before moving on to the next level. The first level is the learner stage (Class 7) which lasts a minimum of 12 months. The next level, stage two, is the probationary (Class 5-GDL) stage which lasts a minimum of 2 years. The process takes a minimum of 3 years to complete. If, however, you obtain your learner licence at the age of 14, the GDL process will take 4 years to complete.

Learner (Class 7)

For this level, you must be 14 years old or older, pass a vision screening test and pass a knowledge test of the rules of the road. If you have a medical condition that can impact safe driving, you must provide a medical form that has been filled out by your doctor. If you are under 18 years of age you must have parental or a guardian's consent. You must also bring valid identification with you when taking any tests.

Use this study guide (and other sources) to help you prepare for your knowledge test. If you pass, you will obtain your learner Class 7 licence. Knowledge tests and vision screening tests are done with an Alberta registry agent. Find the location nearest you at: www.servicealberta.ca/1641.cfm.

You do not need to make an appointment for the knowledge test or vision screening test. Ensure you have adequate time to perform the tests. Centre hours may vary.

Once you get your Class 7 licence you must follow a number of learner conditions at this level or risk suspension of your licence. See "conditions" on page 6. **Please note: Laws and therefore driving "conditions" may change. Consult other sources for the most up-to-date information.**

GDL Probationary (Class 5)

You must have your learner's licence for 12 months before trying for the Class 5 GDL Probationary licence. Once you have developed enough practice with a coach at the learner level you can book your first road test. You must be at least 16 years old to take the Alberta Class 5 road test.

To take your first road test, buy a test permit from a licensed driver examiner or from a registry agent. Appointments can be made in person at these places.

You will be tested on basic driving skills which can include: stopping, turning right or left, changing lanes, parking, obeying traffic signs or signals and general rules of the road. The road test will take a minimum of 25 minutes.

Ensure you bring the appropriate vehicle for the class of licence being tested and that it is in good working order. The examiner pretest vehicle check includes: properly functioning brake lights, turn signal lights, headlights, seatbelts, all mirrors, enough gas for the test, proper insurance, valid licence plates, etc.

If you pass the first road test, you will be a probationary driver with a Class 5-GDL licence and you will have more driving privileges than at the learner level. However, you must follow a new set of conditions to ensure your licence is not suspended.

See "conditions" on page 6. **Please note: Laws and therefore driving "conditions" may change. Consult other sources for the most up-to-date information.**

Class 5

If you have had your probationary licence for at least 2 years and have been suspension free for the past year, you can book an advanced road test to obtain a Class 5 operator licence. The advanced road test requires a higher level of driver knowledge than the first road test; 60 hours of driving experience are recommended.

The advanced road test lasts about 60 minutes and covers 20 to 30 kilometres. Ensure your test vehicle is in good working order. Advanced road tests can only be taken at approved locations. For where, consult www.transportation.alberta.ca/.

Learner Conditions	Probationary Conditions
Your blood alcohol level **must be 0** while driving.	Your blood alcohol level **must be 0** while driving.
You **must not drive alone.** You must be accompanied by a fully licensed (non-GDL probationary) driver who is 18 years old or older and they must be in the front seat beside you. They must not be impaired by drugs or alcohol.	You may **not supervise** a learner driver.
You must **not have more passengers** than there are working seatbelts.	You must **not have more passengers** than there are working seatbelts.
You must have a learner licence for at least 1 year.	You must have a probationary licence for at least 2 years.
You will be **suspended at 8 demerit points** versus 15 demerit points for fully licensed drivers.	You will be **suspended at 8 demerit points** versus 15 demerit points for fully licensed drivers.
You must not drive between **midnight and 5:00 a.m.**	You may not upgrade to a commercial licence. This includes Classes 1–4.

Licence Classification Chart

Licence Class		Vehicle Description	Test Minimum Age Requirement
1		Allows any semi-trailer truck and all motor vehicle combinations except motorcycles. For learning only, any Class 6 vehicle.	18
2		Allows buses, school buses, special event buses and all vehicles that holders of a Class 3, 4 or 5 operator's may drive. For learning only, Class 1 and 6.	18
3		Allows a single motor vehicle with three or more axles. This vehicle may tow a trailer that has one or more axles as long as the trailer is not equipped with air brakes. All Class 5 vehicles and combinations included. All Class 2 or 4 vehicles as long as there are no passengers in them. For learning only, all Class 1,2 and 6.	18
4		Allows any bus with a maximum of 24 passengers excluding the driver. Also allows ambulances and taxis. All Class 5 vehicles and combinations included. All Class 1,2,3 and 6 for learning only.	18
5		Allows two-axle single motor vehicles. Recreational vehicles with two or less axles. Two-axle recreational or two-axle motor vehicles may tow a trailer with one or more axles as long as the trailer is not equipped with air brakes. Three-axle recreational vehicle with a trailer not having air brakes and the trailer may have two or less axles. A moped. All Class 2 or 4 vehicles as long as there are no passengers in them. For learning only, includes all motor vehicles in Class 1-4 provided learner is 18 years old. For learning only, a motorcycle.	16
6		Allows motorcycles and mopeds. All Class 5 vehicles and combinations.	16
7		May operate as a learner, all Class 5 vehicles and combinations included. A motorcycle if 16 years old or older and for learning only. A moped.	14

*This licence class chart illustrates typical vehicles allowed in each class. For more detailed information consult the Government of Alberta—Service Alberta (www.servicealberta.gov.ab.ca).

How to Get Your Driver's Licence

1. Bring Personal Identification

If you are a new applicant you will need to show proof of identify to a registry agent before you can apply for an operator's licence. You can only apply for an operator's licence if you are a resident of Alberta. You will need primary photo identification that proves who you are. This identification must show your photo, legal name and date of birth. Support documents are also required and each must contain two of the following: your name, address, date of birth, signature. A registry agent will need to verify all your personal information.

All documents must be valid, not expired and original; no photocopies are allowed.

For a complete list of acceptable documents contact a registry agent office through www.servicealberta.gov.ab.ca .

Some **primary photo identification** examples include:

✔ Passport

✔ Alberta Photo Identification Card

Some **secondary identification** examples include:

✔ Birth Certificate

✔ Credit or Debit Card (as long as the applicant's name is on the card and the applicant has signed the card)

✔ Permanent Resident Card

In addition to the above, there are other documents you may need to bring. These additional documents must contain proof of any missing or invalid information. For example if all primary identification documents are in your maiden name and you are known by your married name, you must bring a marriage certificate to link you to your primary identification.

2. Come with Parental Consent

While you need to be 14 years old or older to enter the GDL program and obtain a learner operator licence, you must bring a custodial parent or guardian with you if you are under 18 years of age. They will need to sign their consent on the licence application. Proof of guardianship or parenthood must be shown. The parent must show valid identification while the 14-year-old may show a birth certificate. You may be able to forego this requirement if you do not live with a parent or guardian or prove you are married.

3. Go to a Registry Agent Office

Bring all required identification, a parent or guardian (if required), fees and glasses if you need them for reading or driving to your nearest registry agent office.

Ensure you arrive well in advance of office closing hours.

4. Pay the Required Fees

All fees are posted online at: www.servicealberta.ca/pdf/registries/Product_Catalogue.pdf . For example, the knowledge test fee is $17. If you pass you may want to purchase your learner operator licence; a 5-year first application fee is $84. All applicable taxes are extra. Since you must have a learner licence for a minimum of 1 year, it is advisable to purchase your learner operator licence as soon as you pass the knowledge test. This is so that you do not lose any time. Your 1-year minimum learner requirement occurs after you have a learner operator licence, not when you pass the knowledge test.

5. Take the Knowledge Test

Your knowledge of what you learned from this study guide and from other sources will be tested on the knowledge test. The knowledge test is an electronic test. You will be given enough time to complete the test but arrive at least 1 hour before business close.

You will have 30 multiple-choice questions which will include traffic signs, traffic control signals, pavement markings and driving related questions. You must answer 25 questions correctly to pass and obtain your learner's licence.

6. Pass a Vision Screening Test and Medical Obligation

You will take a vision test to ensure you see well enough to drive. If you require glasses to drive, this will be noted on your driver's licence with a "condition" code. It is your responsibility and legal obligation to provide a medical report if your health may potentially impact your safe driving ability.

If you are 75 years old or older and you are renewing your licence or applying for an operator's licence you must take a vision screening test. You also have to provide a completed medical report signed by your doctor.

New Residents from Out of Province or Out of Country

If you have a valid driver's licence from another province, state, or country you can drive in Alberta for up to 90 days as a new resident of Alberta.

Within 90 days you must apply for an Alberta operator's licence. You must surrender your old licence as it is illegal to have more than one licence. Other requirements, such as minimum age, may apply depending on where the previous home jurisdiction was.

A valid licence from Austria, Belgium, England, France, Germany, Japan, Republic

of Korea, Scotland, Switzerland, United States, Wales or any country in which Alberta has a Reciprocal Licensing Agreement with, may be exchanged for a Class 5 licence of the same class. Some conditions apply.

For all other countries, even without previous driving document validation, a person may apply to have their previous driving experience credited to their Alberta driving record. Once an application is successful the applicant will have an alternative to the three-year GDL program. Find out more from a registry agent office.

Visitors from Out of Province or Out of Country

If you are visiting Alberta from another province and have a valid driver's licence from your home jurisdiction and a valid address, you may drive in Alberta as

long as you do not take up residency in Alberta. This applies to full-time students, co-op working students and people working in Alberta.

If you are visiting Alberta from a country outside of Canada and have an International Driving Permit (IDP) from your country, you may drive in Alberta for up to 12 months. You must, however, have a valid licence from your home jurisdiction. Find out more from a registry agent office.

Sample Test

Could you pass?

Use the Practice Test Form on pages 101–102 to record your answers and then check the inside back cover to see how well you scored.

ⓘ For each question, select the most appropriate response, without looking below at the added information section. These information boxes sometimes give the answer away. Other times they will provide you with valuable added information to help with your understanding.

Traffic Signs

1.
  a) No stopping.
  b) Stop if necessary and go when intersection is clear.
  c) Come to a complete stop.
  d) Do not enter road.

> (i) If there is no stop line, crosswalk or sidewalk, stop within 3 m of the intersecting roadway.

2.
  a) You have the right-of-way.
  b) Give others the right-of-way.
  c) Always stop, then yield.
  d) Do not enter.

> (i) Traffic or pedestrians in the intersection or close to it have the right-of-way and go first. Only stop if necessary.

3.
  a) The minimum speed you can drive in any condition.
  b) The maximum speed you can drive in any condition.
  c) The minimum speed you can drive in favourable conditions.
  d) The maximum speed you can drive in favourable conditions.

> (i) Reduce speed in traffic or in poor driving conditions. Speed limits are only maximums for ideal conditions.

4.
  a) The speed limit is 50 km/h.
  b) The speed limit is 50 km/h ahead.
  c) It is 50 km to the next rest area.
  d) The speed limit is 50 km/h for a distance of 50 km.

> (i) The speed limit ahead is changing to 50 km/h.

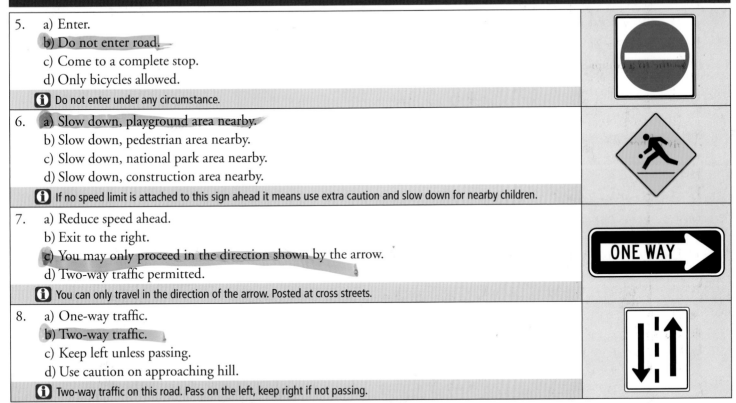

5. a) Enter.
   b) Do not enter road.
   c) Come to a complete stop.
   d) Only bicycles allowed.

   ⓘ Do not enter under any circumstance.

6. a) Slow down, playground area nearby.
   b) Slow down, pedestrian area nearby.
   c) Slow down, national park area nearby.
   d) Slow down, construction area nearby.

   ⓘ If no speed limit is attached to this sign ahead it means use extra caution and slow down for nearby children.

7. a) Reduce speed ahead.
   b) Exit to the right.
   c) You may only proceed in the direction shown by the arrow.
   d) Two-way traffic permitted.

   ⓘ You can only travel in the direction of the arrow. Posted at cross streets.

8. a) One-way traffic.
   b) Two-way traffic.
   c) Keep left unless passing.
   d) Use caution on approaching hill.

   ⓘ Two-way traffic on this road. Pass on the left, keep right if not passing.

9. a) There is an intersection ahead on the right.
   b) Stay to the left of the island or divider.
   c) Stay to the right of the island or divider.
   d) The road curves to the left for 1 km.

   (i) You must keep to the right of the divider ahead.

10. a) No parking to the right of the sign.
    b) No parking to the left of the sign.
    c) No parking anytime.
    d) Parking available on weekends only.

    (i) A prohibitive parking sign. The arrow on the sign indicates where parking is not allowed.

11. a) No bicycles allowed.
    b) This is a bicycle route.
    c) School zone ahead.
    d) Do not watch for bicycles.

    (i) A prohibitive bicyle symbol. For everyone's safety bicycle riding is not allowed after this point.

12. a) Turn right only on a red light.
    b) No right turn ever.
    c) No right turn allowed on a red light.
    d) Do not enter.

    (i) A prohibitive right turn symbol. If the traffic light is red at an intersection you may not turn right.

13. a) Do not pass on this road.
    b) You may pass on this road.
    c) Two-way traffic ahead.
    d) Do not enter.

ⓘ A prohibitive passing symbol. For safety reasons there is no passing on this roadway.

14. a) No trucks allowed.
    b) Motorized snow vehicles allowed.
    c) No motorized snow vehicles allowed.
    d) None of the above.

ⓘ A prohibitive access sign. Motorized snow vehicles are not allowed.

15. a) You are going the wrong way.
    b) You are not going the wrong way.
    c) One-way street ahead so ensure you do not go the wrong way.
    d) You have parked your vehicle the wrong way.

ⓘ Wrong way signs are usually posted on exit ramps to warn you that traffic is oncoming. Do not enter these areas.

16. a) School zone ahead, speed limit is 50 km/h.
    b) School zone ahead does not have a crossing guard.
    c) School zone has ended and you may resume a speed limit of 50 km/h.
    d) School zone has begun and you may drive a speed limit of 50 km/h.

ⓘ The end of a school zone is indicated when a sign says it has ended or an increase in the speed limit is posted.

17 . a) School zone, reduce speed to 60 km/h.
   b) Slow down, school zone nearby, watch for children and drive with extra caution.
   c) You are approaching a school bus loading zone.
   d) Watch for pedestrians at crosswalk.

 (i) School zone signs with attached speed limits (sign at left) indicate you are in a school zone as opposed to a school zone being nearby (sign at right). You must obey the posted speed limits. The speed limit is 30 km/h in rural and urban school zones. Speed limits are in effect only during school days, from 8:00 a.m.–9:30 a.m., 11:30 a.m.–1:30 p.m. and from 3:00 p.m.–4:30 p.m. Hours can vary by municipality and these altered times must be posted. No passing is permitted during school zone hours.

18.   a) Reduce speed to 50 km/h in approaching school zone.
   b) Reduce speed to 30 km/h in approaching school zone.
   c) You must yield to pedestrians crossing the pedestrian crosswalk.
   d) Slow down and proceed with caution at approaching busy intersection.

(i) Yield to all pedestrians crossing the roadway.

19.   a) School crosswalk.
   b) Hidden school bus stop.
   c) Children must be accompanied by an adult in this area.
   d) Intersection ahead.

(i) Watch for children and/or any pedestrians crossing. If present, follow the directions of the school crossing guard.

20. a) If you are in lanes 1, 2 or 3 you have to follow the direction of the arrow.
    b) If you are in lane 1 you may go straight and left.
    c) If you are in lane 2 you may go in any direction.
    d) If you are in lane 3, you may go straight or turn right.

ⓘ Always check signs and pavement markings to ensure you are in the correct lane for turning or going straight.

21. a) Lane is not for left turns.
    b) Lane is only for two-way left turns.
    c) Turn left or right.
    d) No U-turn.

ⓘ This left-turn lane control sign allows vehicles travelling in either direction to turn left from a single shared lane.

22. a) Two right lanes allow drivers to proceed straight.
    b) Two right lanes allow drivers to only turn right.
    c) Two left lanes allow drivers to turn left, right lane allows right turns.
    d) Two left lanes allow drivers to turn left, right lane also allows drivers to go straight.

ⓘ Using correct lanes before or after a turn is critical if vehicles can turn in the same direction from more than 1 lane.

23. a) Two right lanes allow drivers to proceed straight.
    b) Two right lanes allow drivers only to turn right.
    c) Two left lanes allow drivers only to turn left.
    d) Two left lanes allow drivers to turn left, right lane also allows drivers to go straight.

ⓘ Using correct lanes before or after a turn is critical if vehicles can turn in the same direction from more than 1 lane.

24. a) You are only allowed to proceed straight through.
    b) You are not allowed to proceed straight.
    c) Only left and right turns permitted.
    d) Stop at the intersection ahead.

ⓘ A permissive straight through only symbol. You may proceed straight through the intersection.

25. a) Passing is not allowed.
    b) Passing is allowed.
    c) Do not pass emergency vehicles.
    d) Two-lane highway ends.

ⓘ A permissive passing symbol. Pass when it is safe to do so.

26. a) Motorized snow vehicles are allowed on this route or roadway.
    b) Bicycles are allowed on this route or roadway.
    c) This roadway or route allows trucks.
    d) This roadway or route does not allow trucks.

ⓘ A permissive truck route symbol. Be prepared to share the road.

27. a) Passing is not allowed.
    b) Passing is allowed.
    c) Do not pass emergency vehicles.
    d) This route or roadway allows dangerous goods to be transported on it.

ⓘ A permissive dangerous goods route symbol. Be cautious and be prepared to share the road.

28.   a) Left turn permitted.
     b) No left turn permitted.
     c) Left turn allowed after 5:00 p.m.
     d) No left turn on Saturday or Sunday.

ⓘ A prohibitive left turn sign. Unless otherwise indicated proceed straight or right but not left.

29.   a) Parking allowed on either side of the signs.
     b) Parking available after 6:00 p.m.
     c) No parking allowed in direction indicated by arrows.
     d) There is parking available on either side of the arrows.

ⓘ A prohibitive parking sign. No parking between signs unless loading/unloading people or merchandise.

30.   a) No pedestrians are allowed.
     b) Pedestrians are allowed.
     c) Crosswalk ahead.
     d) School zone ahead.

ⓘ A prohibitive pedestrian sign. Pedestrians are not allowed on the roadway.

31.   a) No left turn.
     b) You may go in the opposite direction.
     c) No U-turns allowed.
     d) Turning allowed after 6:00 p.m.

ⓘ A prohibitive turning sign. You may not make a U-turn on this roadway.

32. a) No parking anytime.
    b) No parking during days and times shown.
    c) You can only park after 3:00 p.m. on weekdays.
    d) No parking on weekends.

ⓘ A prohibitive parking sign that does not allow parking during the days and times shown.

33. a) A part-time reserved lane for buses and taxis.
    b) A full-time reserved lane for buses and taxis.
    c) Lanes are for pedestrians only, no vehicles permitted during days and times posted.
    d) Lanes are for loading and unloading passengers only during days and times posted.

ⓘ A reserved lane sign for buses and taxis during peak traffic times of 07:00–09:00 and from 16:00–18:00, Monday to Friday inclusive.

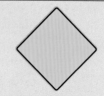

ⓘ Reserved lanes can also be for bicycles, as shown on the sign at left. Some municipalities also have reserved lanes for high occupancy vehicles (HOV) whereby 2 or more occupants in a vehicle are permitted in the reserved lane. When times are indicated on a reserved lane sign for either a bus, taxi, bicycle or vehicles with 2 or more occupants, then the lane is reserved on a part-time basis. If no time is specified then the lane is for full-time use. Reserved lane signs are hung over or beside lanes and a sign will indicate when the reserved lane has ended. All traffic moves in the same direction if a white diamond is against a black background.

34. a) A yellow diamond traffic sign represents a school area.
    b) A yellow diamond traffic sign represents lane designation.
    c) A yellow diamond traffic sign represents construction area.
    d) A yellow diamond traffic sign represents a warning.

ⓘ Traffic signs use standardized shapes, colours and symbols to help drivers recognize what a sign means.

35. a) Hidden left turn ahead.
      b) Hidden crosswalk ahead.
      c) There is a 3-way stop ahead that is hidden.
      d) There is a hidden side road ahead.

ⓘ Drivers on the hidden road may not see traffic from the main road. Proceed with caution toward the "T" intersection.

36. a) Winding road ahead.
      b) Hidden intersection ahead.
      c) Turn right at bridge ahead.
      d) Road turns or bends to the right sharply ahead.

ⓘ The road has a single turn only option as the road changes and bends sharply to the right.

37. a) The road bends to the right ahead.
      b) The road bends to the left ahead.
      c) One-way traffic ahead.
      d) Right turn only lane ahead.

ⓘ Drive accordingly as the road bends or curves slightly to the right. Use recommended speed only in ideal conditions.

38. a) Hidden intersection ahead.
      b) Two-lane highway begins.
      c) Two lanes are about to merge into one. Driver on the right has the right-of-way.
      d) Two lanes are about to merge into one. Drivers in both lanes are responsible to merge safely.

ⓘ Two lanes are merging into one. Merging is the equal responsibility of drivers in both lanes.

39. a) Divided highway begins. b) Divided highway ends. c) Slower traffic keep to the right. d) No intersection ahead. ⓘ Traffic ahead travels in both directions without a divider, so stay to the right.	
40. a) Road has a bend to the right. b) Road turns sharply to the right. c) Left lane ends ahead. d) Right lane ends ahead. ⓘ The right lane ends ahead and you are required to merge with traffic in the lane to the left, if you are in the right lane.	
41. a) There is a narrow bridge ahead. b) The road narrows ahead. c) Two-lane roadway ends. d) Merge with oncoming traffic. ⓘ The roadway will become narrower ahead on both sides.	
42. a) The road has one lane ahead. b) The two-way road curves ahead. c) A narrow passage is ahead. d) Slower traffic move to the right. ⓘ A narrow passage ahead; often a bridge that is narrower than the roadway.	

43. a) Mountain zone ahead.
    b) Bump or uneven or rough road ahead.
    c) Construction zone ahead.
    d) Falling rocks ahead.

    ⓘ Slow down and keep both hands on the steering wheel for best control of your vehicle and to avoid sudden shifts.

44. a) Single occupancy lane.
    b) Road ahead may be slippery.
    c) You are entering a snowbelt area.
    d) Winding road ahead.

    ⓘ The road is slippery when wet. Reduce speed and drive with caution.

45. a) There is a steep hill ahead.
    b) You are in a mountain zone.
    c) Caution, trucks turning.
    d) Construction zone ahead.

    ⓘ The road has a steep hill ahead. Slow down and be prepared to shift into a lower gear to slow down your vehicle.

46. a) Intersection ahead.
    b) Stop sign ahead.
    c) Stop at crosswalk ahead.
    d) School children crossing ahead.

    ⓘ There is a stop sign ahead so slow down.

47. a) Construction zone ahead.
     b) Railroad crossing ahead.
     c) Traffic lights ahead.
     d) City zone ahead.

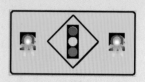

ⓘ You will be approaching a traffic light. If signal lights are flashing be prepared to stop.

48. a) Men at work ahead.
     b) Pedestrian crossing ahead.
     c) School zone ahead.
     d) Obey traffic-control person ahead.

ⓘ Watch for pedestrians at the crossing ahead.

49. a) School crosswalk ahead.
     b) Hidden school bus stop ahead.
     c) Children must be accompanied by an adult in this area.
     d) Intersection ahead.

ⓘ Watch for children crossing and follow the direction of the school safety patrol in their orange vests.

50. a) Railroad tracks ahead.
     b) Hospital ahead. Keep quiet and watch for ambulances.
     c) School crosswalk ahead.
     d) You are approaching a school bus stop ahead.

ⓘ Be very cautious, watch for children and be prepared to stop for a school bus with flashing red lights.

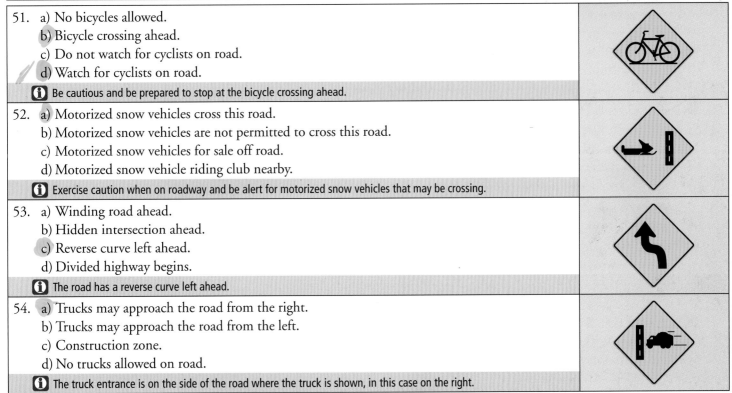

51. a) No bicycles allowed.
  b) Bicycle crossing ahead.
  c) Do not watch for cyclists on road.
  d) Watch for cyclists on road.

ⓘ Be cautious and be prepared to stop at the bicycle crossing ahead.

52. a) Motorized snow vehicles cross this road.
  b) Motorized snow vehicles are not permitted to cross this road.
  c) Motorized snow vehicles for sale off road.
  d) Motorized snow vehicle riding club nearby.

ⓘ Exercise caution when on roadway and be alert for motorized snow vehicles that may be crossing.

53. a) Winding road ahead.
  b) Hidden intersection ahead.
  c) Reverse curve left ahead.
  d) Divided highway begins.

ⓘ The road has a reverse curve left ahead.

54. a) Trucks may approach the road from the right.
  b) Trucks may approach the road from the left.
  c) Construction zone.
  d) No trucks allowed on road.

ⓘ The truck entrance is on the side of the road where the truck is shown, in this case on the right.

Traffic Signs

55. a) A concealed road. b) A "T" intersection. c) A "Y" intersection. d) Railway crossing ahead. ⓘ The "Y" intersection sign warns you that the road branches to the right and left ahead.	
56. a) Paved road ends ahead. b) Gravel road ends ahead. c) One-way road ahead. d) Road ends ahead. ⓘ The paved road ends ahead and is replaced by a gravel road. Reduce speed accordingly.	
57. a) Warning—construction zone ahead. b) You have reached a dead end. c) Road is very bumpy ahead. d) Danger—waterfall behind sign. ⓘ The road ahead does not continue because you have reached a dead end.	
58. a) No animals allowed. b) Watch for deer or other animals crossing the road. c) You are entering a game farm. d) Watch for deer hunters. ⓘ Deer and other animals may cross the road in this area. Slow down and be aware of your surroundings.	

59. a) Railway crossing ahead.
   b) A "T" intersection.
   c) A "Y" intersection.
   d) A concealed road left.

ⓘ There is a concealed road on your left so the sign warns you of vehicles that may be entering the roadway ahead.

60. a) Watch for fallen rocks on road ahead.
   b) Steep hill shift into lower gear.
   c) Construction zone ahead.
   d) Large hailstone area.

ⓘ There could be a landslide or rocks could be falling so drive carefully and be prepared to avoid an accident.

61. a) Truck weigh station ahead.
   b) Sharp turn ahead.
   c) Hazard marker.
   d) Single lane ahead.

ⓘ Downward lines indicate which side to pass hazard on. In this case keep right, hazard object is on the left.

62. a) Hidden intersection ahead.
   b) Added lane ahead.
   c) Two lanes are about to merge into one. Driver on the right has the right-of-way.
   d) Two lanes are about to merge into one. Drivers in both lanes are responsible to merge safely.

ⓘ Lanes can be added where space and traffic allow.

63. a) A winding road is ahead.
    b) Sharp turn in the road ahead.
    c) Hazard to the right.
    d) Hazard to the left.

    ℹ️ The road is winding ahead which may obstruct your ability to see other vehicles.

64. a) The road detours for 6 km until you come to the regular road.
    b) Follow the detour or take the regular road.
    c) Merge with road that closed.
    d) Lane closed ahead. Slow down and merge with traffic.

    ℹ️ Follow this sign through the detour until you come to the regular road.

65. a) Survey crew working on road.
    b) Road closed ahead.
    c) People working ahead.
    d) Uneven pavement ahead.

    ℹ️ Obey all posted construction speed limits at all times. If people are working fines are doubled.

66. a) Flag person controlling traffic ahead.
    b) Uneven pavement ahead.
    c) Survey crew assessing road ahead.
    d) Construction zone ends.

    ℹ️ Slow down and obey instructions from the flag person ahead.

67. a) Movie filming set.
    b) Sightseeing binoculars ahead.
    c) Survey crew ahead.
    d) Bird watchers ahead.

ⓘ Use caution as surveyors may be near the road. Obey all posted speed limits.

68. a) Construction zone begins.
    b) Construction zone ends.
    c) Construction zone ends and detour begins.
    d) Road detours for 6 km.

ⓘ The construction zone has ended and you may resume the regular posted speed limit.

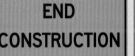

69. a) Speed in area is very slow, less than 40 km/h.
    b) Slow moving vehicle on road travelling less than 40 km/h.
    c) Snow removal vehicle ahead.
    d) Danger, keep out, road under construction.

ⓘ All vehicles moving less than 40 km/h must display a slow moving vehicle sign at rear if driving on a road.

70. a) Winding road ahead.
    b) Bump ahead.
    c) Falling rock ahead.
    d) Uneven pavement ahead.

ⓘ Road construction has resulted in the pavement being uneven so use caution, reduce speed and be prepared to stop.

71. a) Indicates which direction to go for the city or town posted.
    b) Indicates distance, in kilometres, to the city or town posted.
    c) Indicates the distance to campgrounds and green conservation areas.
    d) Indicates by distance shown that Edmonton is before Calgary.

    ⓘ Sign tells you the distance, in kilometres, to the city or town posted. Helps with rest stops and gas planning.

    | Calgary | 20 km |
    | Edmonton | 314 km |

72. a) Indicates which direction to go for the city or town posted.
    b) All towns or cities posted on this sign are 50 km away.
    c) Construction ahead so be prepared to detour by direction shown.
    d) Indicates there is provincial park in the city or town posted.

    ⓘ This information sign tells you in which direction you must travel to get to the city or town posted.

    ↑ Red Deer
    ← Sundre
    Hanna →

73. a) Indicates you are driving in Manitoba.
    b) Indicates there is an exit in 1 km.
    c) Indicates provincial park ahead.
    d) Route marker to indicate you are on the Trans-Canada Highway in Alberta.

    ⓘ You can travel from the east coast of Canada all the way to Victoria, B.C. by following Trans-Canada highway signs.

    TRANS CANADA 1 ALBERTA

74. a) Indicates there is a gas station nearby.
    b) Shows what services are offered 100 km ahead.
    c) Shows what services are not available nearby or off-road.
    d) Shows what services are located nearby or off-road.

    ⓘ Indicates what services are available off-road or nearby. Can include some or all of these.

    ✈ H P

75. a) Indicates there is an airport nearby.
    b) Shows what facilities are offered 100 km ahead.
    c) Shows what facilities are not available nearby or off-road.
    d) Shows what facilities are located nearby or off-road.

ℹ️ Indicates what off-road facilities are available nearby. Can include campgrounds, telephone, police, etc.

76. a) Roadway allows for wide loads.
    b) Heavy construction trucks will be in area.
    c) Wide load being driven.
    d) Road widening occurring.

ℹ️ Used at the back of vehicles transporting a wide load. Use extra caution when passing these vehicles.

77. a) This is a pedestrian crosswalk.
    b) A railway crossing is X-shaped and filled in with red.
    c) Deer cross this area.
    d) A railway crossing sign indicating railway tracks cross the road.

ℹ️ Trains could be approaching so look both ways and be prepared to stop.

78. a) Bridge ahead.
    b) Bridge flooding ahead.
    c) Railway crossing ahead.
    d) Deer tracks ahead.

ℹ️ A warning there is a railway crossing ahead so slow down and be prepared to stop.

79. a) Flashing red lights and lowered gate are a railway crossing warning to drive slow.
    b) Flashing red lights and lowered gate indicate to proceed slowly across the tracks.
    c) Flashing red lights and lowered gate indicate to stop and wait at the railway crossing.
    d) Flashing red lights and lowered gate indicate to drive around the gate or barrier.

ⓘ Stop at least 5 m back and not more than 15 m from nearest rail, gate or barrier. Only cross tracks when gates are raised, lights have stopped flashing and bells have stopped ringing.

80. a) No stopping except to unload passengers.
    b) There is a stop sign ahead.
    c) Come to a complete stop.
    d) No stopping at any time between no-stopping signs.

ⓘ A prohibitive stopping symbol. Besides no stopping, you are not allowed to load or unload passengers between signs that look like this.

81. a) Construction zone, reduce speed to 30 km/h.
    b) National park zone, reduce speed to 30 km/h.
    c) Pedestrian zone, reduce speed to 30 km/h.
    d) Playground zone, reduce speed to 30 km/h.

ⓘ Unless otherwise posted the speed limit in both urban and rural playground zones is 30 km/h. This speed is in effect daily from 8:30 a.m. to 1 hour after sunset. There is also no passing permitted during playground zone hours.

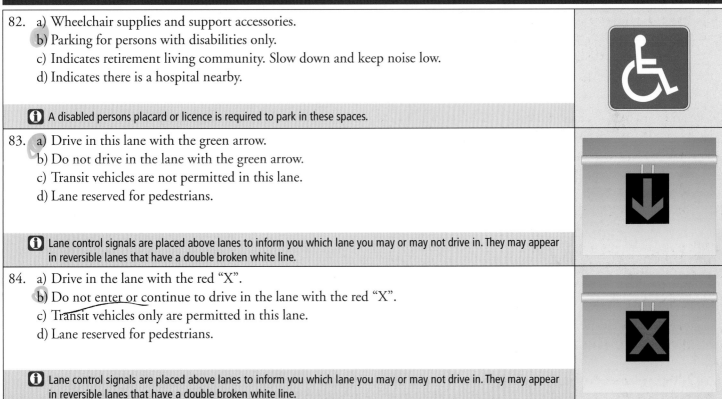

82. a) Wheelchair supplies and support accessories.
     b) Parking for persons with disabilities only.
     c) Indicates retirement living community. Slow down and keep noise low.
     d) Indicates there is a hospital nearby.

ⓘ A disabled persons placard or licence is required to park in these spaces.

83. a) Drive in this lane with the green arrow.
     b) Do not drive in the lane with the green arrow.
     c) Transit vehicles are not permitted in this lane.
     d) Lane reserved for pedestrians.

ⓘ Lane control signals are placed above lanes to inform you which lane you may or may not drive in. They may appear in reversible lanes that have a double broken white line.

84. a) Drive in the lane with the red "X".
     b) Do not enter or continue to drive in the lane with the red "X".
     c) Transit vehicles only are permitted in this lane.
     d) Lane reserved for pedestrians.

ⓘ Lane control signals are placed above lanes to inform you which lane you may or may not drive in. They may appear in reversible lanes that have a double broken white line.

Traffic Control Signals

85. a) Speed up and clear the intersection so you do not block traffic when the light changes. b) Slow down and proceed with caution only if you cannot stop in time; otherwise stop at the appropriate markings. c) Keep going and do not stop as another car can hit you from behind. d) There is road construction ahead so slow down and proceed with caution.	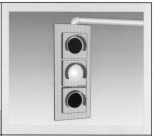

ⓘ Stop safely if you can, otherwise proceed with caution. Amber lights are meant for clearing intersections safely.

86. a) Slow down and drive with caution. b) Stop and proceed when it is safe. c) Stop and turn left. d) Stop and turn right.	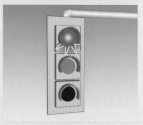

ⓘ Bring your vehicle to a complete stop at a flashing red light. Proceed into the intersection only when safe to do so.

87. a) Slow down and proceed with caution. b) Stop and proceed when it is safe. c) Stop and turn left. d) Stop and turn right.	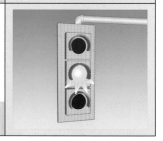

ⓘ Flashing amber lights warn you to slow down and proceed cautiously. Always yield to pedestrians and other vehicles in the intersection.

88.
a) You have the right-of-way to go in any direction in the intersection from the correct lane.
b) A flashing green light means only vehicles turning right may do so.
c) A flashing green light means only vehicles turning left may do so.
d) None of the above.

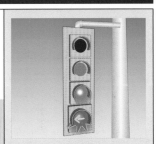

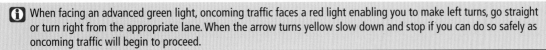
ⓘ When facing an advanced green light, oncoming traffic faces a red light enabling you to make left turns, go straight or turn right from the appropriate lane. When the arrow turns yellow slow down and stop if you can do so safely as oncoming traffic will begin to proceed.

89.
a) Proceed straight or turn right or left.
b) Stop and proceed when it is safe.
c) Stop and turn left.
d) Stop and turn right.

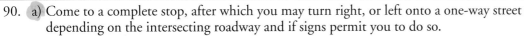
ⓘ A steady green light permits you to go straight, turn left or turn right unless prohibited through a sign or lights. Vehicles turning must yield the right-of-way to pedestrians and other vehicles.

90.
a) Come to a complete stop, after which you may turn right, or left onto a one-way street depending on the intersecting roadway and if signs permit you to do so.
b) From a one-way street to a one-way street you may turn left after slowing for a red light.
c) If you are in a hurry you may drive through red lights with caution only if the way is clear.
d) All of the above.

ⓘ You must always come to a complete stop at the appropriate road markings or intersection edge on a red light before making any turns.

91. a) Pedestrians may cross the road and have right-of-way over vehicles.
b) Pedestrians may cross the road but must yield right-of-way to vehicles.
c) Stop and yield the right-of-way to vehicles.
d) Cross the intersection in any direction.

ℹ Pedestrians may proceed in the direction of the light where a walking symbol or the word "Walk" may appear.

92. a) Flashing amber lights when used with other symbols means reduce speed to 50 km/h.
b) Flashing amber lights when used with other symbols means reduce speed to 40 km/h.
c) Flashing amber lights when used with other symbols means reduce speed to 30 km/h.
d) Flashing amber lights when used with other symbols means reduce speed to 20 km/h.

ℹ Sometimes flashing amber lights are combined with school crossing, pedestrian crossing, school zone signs, etc. and you must yield right-of-way to pedestrians and you must slow down to 30 km/h.

93. a) Only the blue car may pass when the way is clear.
b) Only the red car may pass when the way is clear.
c) No cars may pass when the way is clear.
d) Both cars may pass when the way is clear.

ℹ Broken yellow lines to the left in your lane mean you may pass when the way is clear. A solid yellow line to the left of a broken line means you may still pass when clear but vehicles in the opposite direction may not.

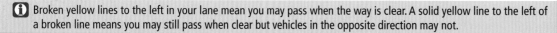

94. a) The car on the right may pass when the way is clear.
    b) The car on the left may pass when the way is clear.
    c) Both cars may pass in either direction when the way is clear.
    d) None of the above.

ⓘ Broken yellow lines mean you may pass when the way is clear in a safe passing area.

95. a) The car on the right may pass when the way is clear.
    b) The car on the left may pass when the way is clear.
    c) Neither car may pass in any direction when outside of urban areas.
    d) All of the above.

ⓘ A single solid or double solid yellow line, outside of an urban area, means you may not pass.

96. a) A left turn lane in the centre for those travelling north.
    b) A left turn lane in the centre for those travelling south.
    c) An extra lane for driving in.
    d) A two-way left turn lane in the centre for traffic going in either direction.

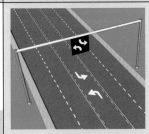

ⓘ Two-way left turn lanes are meant to be shared by traffic going in both directions.

97. a) Either vehicle may change lanes when it is safe to do so.
    b) No vehicles may change lanes.
    c) Slower vehicles must keep left.
    d) None of the above.

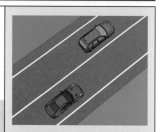

ⓘ Unlike yellow lines separating traffic in opposite directions, white lines separate traffic moving in the same direction. A solid white line indicates you may not change lanes.

98. a) Reserved lane ahead.
    b) Paved road ends and gravel road begins.
    c) A pedestrian crosswalk.
    d) School zone ahead.

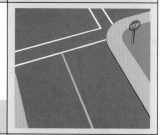

ⓘ Intersections having two parallel white lines denote a pedestrian crosswalk. Multiple vertical lines are also used at intersections or railway crossings. In either case, motorists are to stop at the appropriate markings.

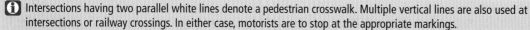
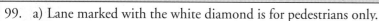

99. a) Lane marked with the white diamond is for pedestrians only.
    b) Lane marked with the white diamond is for loading and unloading passengers only.
    c) Lane marked with the white diamond is only for 5 or more passengers.
    d) Lane marked with the white diamond is only for specific vehicles indicated on signing.

ⓘ Lanes reserved for specific vehicles are marked with a white diamond. Signing on the roadway will indicate what the permitted vehicles are and if there are any days of the week and/or time restrictions.

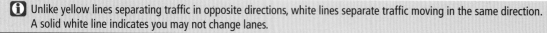
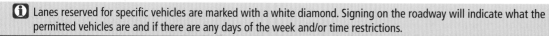

100. a) Yellow markings act as warnings to keep to the right of a painted island.
 b) Yellow markings act as left and right turn lane guides.
 c) Yellow markings provide drivers information about upcoming exits.
 d) Yellow markings indicate to slow down and turn left on these markings.

ℹ️ Steer clear of solid painted road markings that are around fixed objects or act as a painted island. Ensure you do not pass in them or drive over them.

101. a) You are approaching a crosswalk.
 b) You are approaching a railway crossing.
 c) You are approaching a fire station.
 d) None of the above.

ℹ️ Pavement "X" markings warn you of an approaching railway crossing.

102. a) The red and blue car may change lanes when it is safe to do so.
 b) The red and blue car may not change lanes.
 c) Only the red car may change lanes when it is safe to do so.
 d) Only the blue car may change lanes when it is safe to do so.

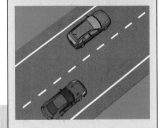

ℹ️ Broken white lines indicate you may change lanes.

103. When are you required to wear a seatbelt?
   a) Wearing a seatbelt is optional.
   b) Only drivers are required to wear a seatbelt.
   c) Only passengers are required to wear a seatbelt.
   d) All drivers and passengers are required to wear a seatbelt and be properly secured.

ⓘ Drivers will receive a fine for not wearing a seatbelt. Drivers must ensure all passengers under the age of 16 are properly secured. Passengers 16 years and older can also be fined for not wearing a seatbelt.

104. What does the law state about seatbelts and children?
   a) All children under 8 years old must be in a booster seat.
   b) All children under 8 years old must be in a rear-facing child car seat.
   c) All children under 8 years old must wear protective headgear.
   d) All children under 6 years old and who weigh less than 18 kg must be in a child safety seat.

ⓘ A child's weight and/or age determines what type of car seat is required and children must be correctly restrained

105. Within how many metres of following another vehicle must you dim your high beam headlights?
   a) Within 50 m.
   b) Within 150 m.
   c) Within 1150 m.
   d) They must be seen clearly in the dark.

ⓘ Ensure headlights are on 1 hour after sunset until 1 hour before sunrise.

106. **What is an uncontrolled intersection?**
    a) An intersection with traffic lights.
    b) An intersection with traffic signs and traffic lights.
    c) An intersection without traffic signs or traffic lights.
    d) An intersection with a police officer who is directing traffic.

ⓘ At an uncontrolled intersection a driver must yield to traffic on their right. Be extra cautious at uncontrolled intersections. Drive slowly and be ready to stop.

107. **What should you do when approaching a construction zone?**
    a) Slow down as signs may be posted with reduced speed limits.
    b) Obey all warning signs.
    c) Follow direction of the road construction flag person.
    d) All of the above.

ⓘ Fines for speeding are doubled when workers are present in construction zones.

108. **Unless posted, within an urban area the maximum speed limit is?...**
    a) 40 km/h.
    b) 50 km/h.
    c) 70 km/h.
    d) 80 km/h.

ⓘ The speed limit is 80 km/h outside of urban areas for non-primary highways if no speed limit is posted.

109. **If 2 vehicles come to an uncontrolled intersection at the same time, who has the right-of-way?**
    a) The vehicle on the right.
    b) The vehicle on the left.
    c) The vehicle turning right.
    d) The vehicle turning left.

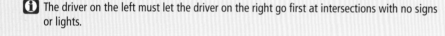 The driver on the left must let the driver on the right go first at intersections with no signs or lights.

110. **If you are turning left at an uncontrolled intersection and a pedestrian is crossing your path, who has the right-of-way?**
    a) You do. Come to a complete stop and make your turn.
    b) Any other car at the intersection that is turning right.
    c) You must yield the right-of-way to approaching traffic and/or to pedestrians crossing.
    d) Whoever is more in a hurry goes first.

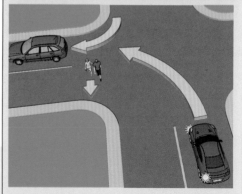

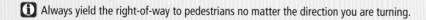 Always yield the right-of-way to pedestrians no matter the direction you are turning.

111. What do the thicker white markings in this diagram represent?

    a) They indicate where you should stop.

    b) They indicate there is a one-way street to the right.

    c) These solid lines indicate there is no passing in either direction.

    d) They do not indicate anything.

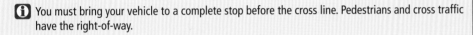

ⓘ You must bring your vehicle to a complete stop before the cross line. Pedestrians and cross traffic have the right-of-way.

112. What is the best way to check for blind spots?

    a) Through your side mirrors.

    b) Through your rear-view mirrors.

    c) Shoulder checks—turning your head and looking through the side windows.

    d) Asking your passengers to check for you.

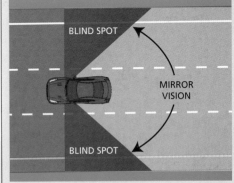

BLIND SPOT

MIRROR VISION

BLIND SPOT

ⓘ Properly adjusted mirrors can help reduce the extent of blind spots. Shoulder checks are the best way to check for blind spots.

113. **Why must you use signals when turning, changing lanes, parking or moving to or from the roadside?**
    a) To inform other drivers of what you want to do.
    b) To inform pedestrians of what you want to do.
    c) To send out an alert of your intentions.
    d) All of the above.

ⓘ Failing to use proper signals can result in a fine and demerit points. Always signal to inform others of your intentions. Using signals allows you to communicate with other vehicles and pedestrians.

114. **If you are facing a red light and a police officer instructs you to go through, what should you do?**
    a) First stop at the intersection and then proceed.
    b) Slow down to 40 km/h and then proceed through the intersection.
    c) Follow the direction of the police officer despite what the traffic light or road sign indicates.
    d) Treat the intersection as a four-way stop.

ⓘ Always follow the direction of a police officer that is directing traffic or face a fine and penalty points.

115. **Winter driving can be very hazardous; how can you best prepare for driving in winter?**
    a) Have a car tune-up.
    b) Ensure you have adequate tread on your tires or switch to snow tires.
    c) Ensure your vehicle's wipers and heat are working well.
    d) All of the above.

ⓘ Ensure you can see through your windshield. It is against the law to have your view blocked by snow, frost, mud, etc.

116. **What 3 factors impact a driver's stopping distance?**
    a) Perception time and reaction time.
    b) Perception time, reaction time and braking time.
    c) Perception time and braking time.
    d) None of the above.

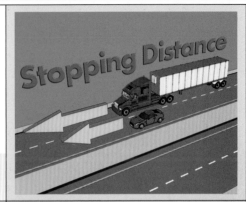

ⓘ Misjudging how long it takes to stop a vehicle can contribute to accidents. Each factor—perception, reaction and braking time—contributes to overall stopping distance.

117. **Coming to a complete stop at the pictured intersection is required, but where do you stop?**
    a) You stop right beside the stop sign.
    b) You stop right after the stop sign.
    c) You stop before the marked crosswalk.
    d) You stop a little into the intersection so that you can see traffic and pedestrians.

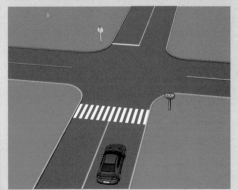

ⓘ You must also wait for the intersection to be clear before entering it.

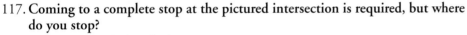
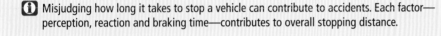

45

118. **Can you make a right turn on a red light?**
    a) Yes, as long as a sign does not tell you otherwise.
    b) Yes, as long as you are in a reserved lane.
    c) No, there are no right turns on red lights allowed in Alberta.
    d) No, there are no right turns on roadways shared with pedestrians.

ⓘ Ensure you first come to a complete stop and that your way is clear before making your turn.

119. **How do you make a left turn from a two-way road onto a two-way road?**
    a) Turn from the right lane into the right curb lane.
    b) Turn from the right lane into the lane right of the centre line.
    c) Turn from the closest lane to the centre line into the right curb lane.
    d) Turn from the closest lane to the centre line into the lane closest to the centre line.

ⓘ Unless otherwise posted left turns are made from the far left lane. Signal, check all directions and ensure way is clear. After turning move into the right curb lane when it is clear to do so.

120. **How much space should you have between you and any vehicle you are following?**

    a) No rule applies and you will not get a fine or demerit points as long as caution is used.

    b) There is a rule of 20 seconds but it is for motorcycle drivers only.

    c) At least 12 seconds so you can see around the vehicle ahead and also have enough time to stop.

    d) At least 2 seconds so you can see around the vehicle ahead and also have enough time to stop.

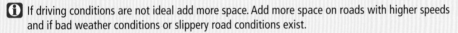
ℹ️ If driving conditions are not ideal add more space. Add more space on roads with higher speeds and if bad weather conditions or slippery road conditions exist.

121. **At a controlled intersection with a four-way stop, when 2 vehicles arrive at the same time, which vehicle may proceed through the intersection first?**

    a) Both vehicles may proceed through the intersection.

    b) The vehicle on the right.

    c) The vehicle on the left.

    d) Both vehicles may go at the same time if they are at right angles to each other.

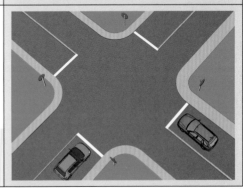

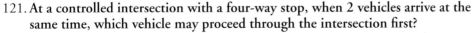
ℹ️ All vehicles are required to come to a complete stop at four-way stop intersections. The vehicle that arrives first is normally the first to go through the intersection. In the circumstance where two vehicles arrive at the same time, then the vehicle on the left must yield to the vehicle on the right.

122. When you come to a railway crossing and there are flashing signal lights, what must you do?

    a) Continue slowly because flashing lights are only a warning to drive slow.

    b) Stop and then proceed slowly across the tracks.

    c) Stop and wait for the signal lights to stop flashing.

    d) Drive around the gate or barrier to avoid getting stuck on the tracks.

ℹ️ Stop at least 5 m back from the nearest rail, gate, or barrier. Only cross tracks once gates rise and lights stop flashing.

123. Where are U-turns not permitted?

    a) In urban areas between intersections.

    b) At intersections controlled by traffic lights.

    c) Outside urban areas on a hill or curve where a driver of another vehicle cannot see you.

    d) All of the above.

ℹ️ U-turns are only advisable when they can be made safely without obstructing other motorists. Watch for signs where U-turns may not be permitted.

124. What vehicle has flashing amber and red lights?

    a) A school bus.

    b) A tow truck.

    c) A snowplow.

    d) An ambulance.

ℹ️ Snow removal vehicles are slow and can be wide. Be cautious when passing them as snow may be blowing and obstructing your view to pass safely. Stay well back and maintain a safe space cushion.

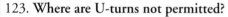

125. **If you approach an intersection that is blocked with traffic what should you do?**
   a) Stop before entering the intersection.
   b) Move up so cars behind you can move forward.
   c) Slowly proceed through the intersection.
   d) Turn left or right to avoid the heavy traffic back-up.

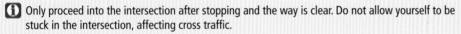

ⓘ Only proceed into the intersection after stopping and the way is clear. Do not allow yourself to be stuck in the intersection, affecting cross traffic.

126. **Why is it dangerous to drive to closely to bicycles?**
   a) Bicycles can achieve a high rate of speed.
   b) Bicycles are not required to adhere to the rules of the road.
   c) Bicycles are not considered a vehicle.
   d) Bicycles do not have brake lights when they stop and you may not be able to stop in time.

ⓘ Always exercise caution around bicycles—leaving adequate stopping space, checking your blind spots before changing lanes or turning and remembering that cyclists have very little protection against the impact of a heavy vehicle.

Driving Responsibly

127. **When 2 vehicles are driving in a traffic circle and vehicle B is in the outside lane and vehicle A is in the inside lane, which vehicle must yield the right of way?**
    a) Neither vehicle has the right-of-way.
    b) Vehicle A has the right of way because in a traffic circle the vehicle on the right is required to yield to the vehicle on the left.
    c) Vehicle B has the right of way because in a traffic circle the vehicle on the left is required to yield to the vehicle on the right.
    d) The vehicle that signals first.

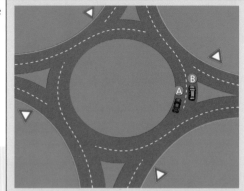

ⓘ In a traffic circle vehicles entering the circle must yield to traffic already in the circle. When in a traffic circle, vehicles on the left have the right of way.

128. **What do intersections controlled by yield signs mean?**
    a) You must always come to a complete stop before proceeding.
    b) The yield signs remind pedestrians to yield right-of-way to vehicles.
    c) Slow down, stop if required to yield right-of-way to traffic or pedestrians; otherwise proceed without stopping.
    d) None of the above.

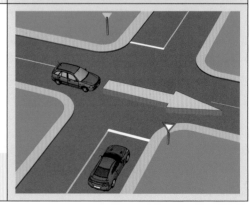

ⓘ Always yield the right-of-way to other traffic and pedestrians, then wait for a safe gap before entering the intersection to proceed.

129. **What should you do if you want to make a right turn?**
  a) Once you are in the correct turning lane, signal left, then turn.
  b) Do a shoulder check to the right to ensure the way is clear.
  c) Ensure you are in the correct turning lane at least 15 m from the intersection.
  d) Both b) and c).

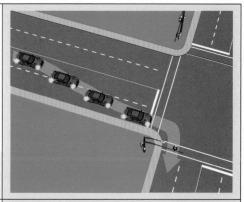

ⓘ Before moving into the correct turning lane always make sure to do a mirror check, shoulder check to determine if it is safe to do so. When it is safe, signal and make the lane change.

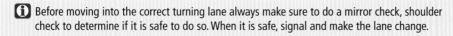

130. **Can you turn left on a red light from a one-way road onto a one-way road?**
  a) Yes, if you signal, stop first in the farthest left lane and then proceed when the way is clear.
  b) Yes, as long as you drive slowly and cautiously.
  c) No left turns are permitted on a red light in Alberta.
  d) Left turns are only permitted from two-way roads to two-way roads on a green light.

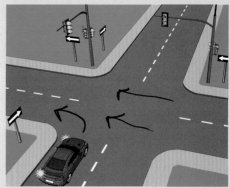

ⓘ Ensure you yield to pedestrians and traffic after first coming to a complete stop.

131. **How do you make a left turn from a two-way road onto a two-lane one-way road?**
    a) Turn from the closest lane to the centre line into the left curb lane.
    b) Turn from the closest lane to the centre line into the right curb lane.
    c) Turn from the far right lane into the left curb lane.
    d) Turn from the right lane into the right curb lane.

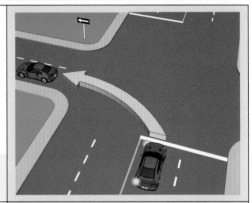

ⓘ Always signal in advance, check all directions and then proceed slowly making a smooth arc.

132. **Why is it a bad idea to turn your steering wheel to the left while waiting to make a left turn at an intersection?**
    a) In case you need to turn right; it will be harder to steer out of the turn.
    b) It is not a bad idea; your vehicle will not be able to make the turn in time if you do not.
    c) Another vehicle can push your vehicle into oncoming traffic.
    d) Turning your steering wheel unnecessarily will add to your car's wear and tear.

ⓘ Keep your wheels straight and avoid getting pushed into oncoming traffic. Only turn your steering wheel to the left when you can make the turn.

133. At what speed should you use the two-second rule for following a vehicle?

a) Any speed.

b) 50 km/h.

c) 80 km/h.

d) 100 km/h.

ⓘ The two-second rule is the minimum distance you should keep between you and the vehicle in front of you. You should increase your following distance during poor weather conditions or when other hazards such as poor road conditions exist.

134. What must your blood alcohol level be if you hold a learner's licence?

a) Less than 1.0.

b) Less than .08.

c) Less than .05.

d) 0.0.

ⓘ You must have a blood alcohol level of 0.0: therefore, no alcohol. GDL violators will automatically get a 1-month suspension under the Alberta Zero Alcohol Tolerance Program (AZAT).

135. Within how many metres of an oncoming vehicle must you dim your highbeam headlights?

a) Within 30 m.

b) Within 300 m.

c) Within 150 m.

d) Within 1150 m.

ⓘ Do not blind other night drivers. Switch from highbeam to lowbeam within 300 m of other oncoming vehicles.

Driving Responsibly

136. **What can car A and B do, based on the arrows?**
   a) Car A or B can go straight or turn left.
   b) Car A must turn left while car B can go straight or turn left.
   c) Car B must turn left while car A can go straight or turn left.
   d) None of the above.

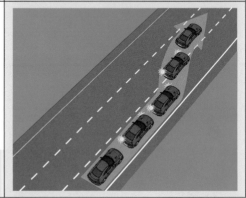

137. **What must you do when entering, pulling into or changing lanes?**
   a) Ensure road markings and signs allow you to change lanes.
   b) Check all mirrors and your blind spot.
   c) Signal and steer into lane safely.
   d) All of the above.

138. When parking uphill beside a curb what should you do?

a) Turn your tires to the left and reverse slightly so the front right tire touches the curb.

b) Turn your tires to the right to catch the curb if your vehicle rolls backward.

c) Make your tires as straight as possible to be parallel with the curb.

d) The direction of your tires does not matter as long as you set the parking brake.

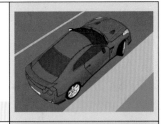

ⓘ It is a good practice to always set your parking brake when your vehicle is parked regardless of terrain.

139. When a driver needs to brake in an emergency situation and their vehicle is equipped with ABS (Anti-lock braking system) what is the proper method of applying the brakes?

a) Remove your foot from the brake completely.

b) Pump the brakes continuously.

c) Apply firm and continuous pressure on the brake pedal.

d) Apply light and continuous pressure on the brake pedal.

ⓘ ABS is activated by hard braking. Pedal "chatter" is an indication that the ABS is working properly so don't be worried by the vibration or noise.

140. Why should a driver exercise caution when in the presence of a pedestrian with a white cane?

a) The pedestrian is not able to hear.

b) A white cane indicates the pedestrian has a visual impairment.

c) The pedestrian is not required to adhere to the rules of the road.

d) Both a) and b).

ⓘ A person with a visual impairment may make an error in navigation. It is important to to be prepared to stop.

141. What are passing or climbing lanes for?

    a) They allow for frequent stops and a rest area ahead.

    b) They are for vehicles that have trouble climbing hills.

    c) They help thin out traffic by providing an extra lane.

    d) They allow slower vehicles to move into the right lane so faster ones can pass on the left.

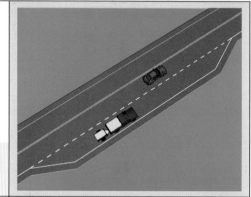

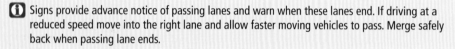

ⓘ Signs provide advance notice of passing lanes and warn when these lanes end. If driving at a reduced speed move into the right lane and allow faster moving vehicles to pass. Merge safely back when passing lane ends.

142. If you are being passed on a two-lane highway what should you do?

    a) Speed up so that the flow of traffic increases.

    b) Move to the left to alert oncoming cars someone is trying to pass in their lane.

    c) Move a little to the right so that the passing vehicle can see ahead and pass you safely.

    d) None of the above.

ⓘ Passing can be dangerous and should be done with extreme caution. Always ensure passing is permitted and that the way is clear far enough ahead to make a pass safely. Perform all necessary checks and double checks using mirrors, shoulder checks, signals and proper lane changes.

143. What should you do when entering a highway?

a) Signal, then stop to wait for an opening in traffic.

b) Time your approach by adjusting your vehicle speed to merge smoothly into the flow of traffic.

c) Signal, then accelerate and enter traffic quickly.

d) Do what the vehicle ahead of you does.

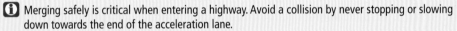 Merging safely is critical when entering a highway. Avoid a collision by never stopping or slowing down towards the end of the acceleration lane.

144. What should you do when exiting a highway?

a) Signal, then stop to wait for an opening in traffic.

b) Check traffic flow, enter acceleration lane, signal and merge smoothly with speed of traffic.

c) Be in the correct lane, signal, move into the deceleration lane, reduce speed gradually and turn off signal.

d) Do what the vehicle ahead of you does.

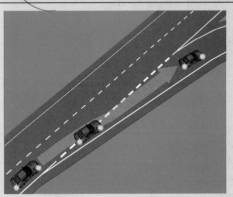

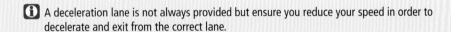 A deceleration lane is not always provided but ensure you reduce your speed in order to decelerate and exit from the correct lane.

145. Under what circumstances are cell phones not allowed while driving?

a) When you use your cell phone to text.

b) When you use your hand-held cell phone to chat.

c) When you use your cell phone to check and send emails.

d) All of the above.

ⓘ Alberta's Distracted Driver legislation restricts drivers from using hand-held cell phones as well as many other restrictions.

146. Which one of these statements is a basic parking rule?

a) Park on a curve or hill so that you can see ahead.

b) Do not park within 5 m of a fire hydrant.

c) Do not park within 150 m of intersections with traffic lights.

d) Do not look while opening your door.

ⓘ Do not block other parked vehicles, sidewalks or roadways. Among other restrictions never park within 5 m of the closest side of a crosswalk, intersection, yield or stop sign.

147. What is important to remember before entering a curve?

a) Reduce speed before entering the curve.

b) Increase speed before entering the curve.

c) Steer shapely to the right when entering a right-hand curve.

d) None of the above.

ⓘ Curves can be very dangerous especially during bad weather or wet road conditions. If vehicle speed is not reduced on entering a curve you may skid out of the curve or your vehicle may tip over.

148. What does the term "over-driving" your headlights mean?

a) You are leaving your lowbeam lights on too long at the risk of burning out the bulbs.

b) You are leaving your highbeam headlights on too long at the risk of burning out the bulbs.

c) You are driving slower than your stopping distance allows you to see.

d) You are driving faster than your stopping distance allows you to see.

ⓘ Slow down while driving at night to ensure you can see far enough ahead to stop appropriately.

149. What should you do while driving when you hear bells, sirens or see flashing emergency vehicle lights?

a) Slow down and move to the far right of the roadway and stop.

b) Slow down and continue slowly in the left lane.

c) Come to a complete stop wherever you are.

d) Speed up and keep the movement of traffic going.

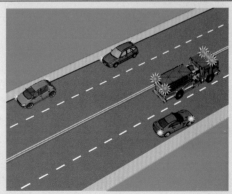

ⓘ Traffic must slow down and stop in the right curb lane on two-way highways or in the nearest curb lane on one-way streets. Stay back 150 m and do not follow emergency vehicles with sirens or lights flashing within 150 m.

150. **Why is it a bad idea to pass on a hill or sharp curve?**
   a) It is not a bad idea as long as you slow down, signal and make a smooth pass.
   b) It is not a bad idea as long as you speed up to ensure you make the pass safely.
   c) It is a bad idea because you can not see far enough ahead or around the curve for potential hazards.
   d) None of the above.

ⓘ Never pass when you are unable to see well enough ahead to assess whether a manoeuvre is safe or not. Passing on a hill or sharp curve can get you a fine and 3 demerit points.

151. **If you want to turn left at an intersection from a one-way street, unless a traffic sign indicates otherwise, which lane should you turn from?**
   a) From the lane closest to the right curb.
   b) From the lane closest to the left curb.
   c) From the lane with the least amount of traffic.
   d) From the centre lane.

ⓘ Plan in advance when making a left turn and be in the proper lane a minimum of 15 m from the intersection you plan to turn from.

152. **What does this hand signal mean?**
   a) Driver in vehicle is slowing down or stopping.
   b) Driver in vehicle is turning right.
   c) Driver in vehicle is turning left.
   d) Driver in vehicle is exiting a highway.

ⓘ If your brake lights or turn signals do not work, or may not be seen, ensure you use proper hand signals to warn other drivers of your intentions. Use both for clarity if in doubt.

153. **What does this hand signal mean?**
   a) Driver in vehicle is slowing down or stopping.
   b) Driver in vehicle is turning right.
   c) Driver in vehicle is turning left.
   d) Driver in vehicle is exiting a highway.

ⓘ If your brake lights or turn signals do not work, or may not be seen, ensure you use proper hand signals to warn other drivers of your intentions. Use both for clarity if in doubt.

154. **What does this hand signal mean?**
   a) Driver in vehicle is slowing down or stopping.
   b) Driver in vehicle is turning right.
   c) Driver in vehicle is turning left.
   d) Driver in vehicle is exiting a highway.

ⓘ If your brake lights or turn signals do not work, or may not be seen, ensure you use proper hand signals to warn other drivers of your intentions. Use both for clarity if in doubt.

Driving Responsibly

155. Which statement is true about passing as you approach a pedestrian crosswalk?

a) You may pass another vehicle at a pedestrian crossing, which has stopped for a pedestrian, as long as you use your signal.

b) You may pass another vehicle at a pedestrian crossing, which has stopped for a pedestrian, as long as you signal and use shoulder checks.

c) You may never pass another vehicle at a pedestrian crossing.

d) Even if there is no pedestrian crossing, it is advisable not to pass another vehicle at a pedestrian crosswalk.

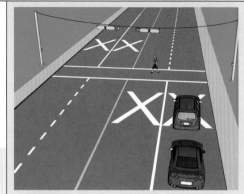

ⓘ Avoid passing other vehicles at an approaching crosswalk. You do not want to prevent drivers from seeing any pedestrians. Passing would obstruct their view.

156. What is the best steering wheel position and how many hands should you use?

a) Use both hands for best control at the 9 and 3 o'clock position.

b) Use both hands for best control at the 11 and 1 o'clock position.

c) Use one hand in any position.

d) Use one hand in the 12 o'clock position.

ⓘ For best control of your vehicle use both hands on the outside of the steering wheel. The 10 o'clock and 2 o'clock position may also be used but the 9 and 3 o'clock position is better if the steering wheel has an air bag; should it go off, your hands have a better chance of staying on the steering wheel.

157. **When do you stop for school buses if there is a median?**
    a) Whenever you approach and see one.
    b) Never because they will stop for you.
    c) Whenever they stop.
    d) Only if you are behind a stopped bus which has its upper red alternating lights flashing.

> ⓘ Remember, if the amber lights are flashing be prepared to stop. These lights act as a warning that the red flashing lights will come on. Some school buses also have flashing stop-sign arms that swing out from the driver's side notifying vehicles to stop. Stop and stay back at least 20 m.

158. **If there is no median, how far in front or behind a stopped school bus, with flashing red lights and stop sign arm extended, are you required to stop?**
    a) At least 20 m—far enough for children to exit the bus and cross safely and for other vehicles to see the red flashing lights.
    b) At least 20 feet—far enough for children to exit the bus and cross safely and for other vehicles to see the red flashing lights.
    c) At least 10 m—far enough for children to exit the bus and cross safely and for other vehicles to see the red flashing lights.
    d) At least 10 feet—far enough for children to exit the bus and cross safely and for other vehicles to see the red flashing lights.

> ⓘ Only proceed when the alternating flashing red lights have been turned off.

159. What should you do if your headlights fail?
a) Turn on your hazard lights and pull to a safe parking area well away from the road.
b) Turn on all your interior lights so that you can see where you are going.
c) Sound your horn to warn others of your problem.
d) All of the above.

ⓘ If headlights fail after attempts to turn them on and off, turn on your hazard lights and move off the road completely.

160. How much time do you have to surrender your operator's licence, insurance and registration when asked to do so by a peace officer?
a) Immediately.
b) Within 12 hours.
c) Within 24 hours.
d) You do not have to, they will look you up in the system.

ⓘ You must present these required documents immediately. Failure to do so can result in a fine.

161. What is the best thing to do if you feel drowsy while driving?
a) Reduce speed.
b) Turn on your heater.
c) Take a nap off the road in a safe area.
d) Keep driving and your drowsiness will pass.

ⓘ Fatigue can impair your judgment and reaction time which could lead to a deadly collision. Ensure you are well-rested and alert before you get behind a steering wheel.

162. **If entering the GDL program, how long must drivers hold a learner's licence before becoming a probationary driver and taking a Class 5 road test?**
   a) 6 months
   b) 12 months
   c) 20 months
   d) 2 years

(i) In the GDL program you must hold a learner's licence for a minimum of 1 year and be at least 16 years of age before applying for the next level.

163. **What are you required to do if a peace officer signals you to pull over?**
   a) Slow down and wait for the officer to pull up beside you for further instructions.
   b) Slow down, safely pull over in the right lane and come to a complete stop.
   c) Stop in the lane you are in.
   d) Signal and stop at the next intersection and wait for the peace officer.

(i) Failing to stop for a peace officer will get you a fine and 5 demerit points.

164. **How many passengers may you have in a vehicle if you have a learner's licence?**
   a) Only the learner driver with a fully licensed driver who is in the backseat of the car.
   b) Up to a maximum of 4.
   c) As many as there are working seatbelts.
   d) No other passengers may be in the car with you.

(i) Passengers must not exceed the number of working seatbelts. Included must be a fully licensed (non-GDL probationary) driver meeting all requirements, who is seated beside the driver.

165. **Which statement is true?**

   a) Licence plates are not transferable from one person to another.
   b) Licence plates are transferable from one person to another.
   c) You have 30 days to register any new vehicle and obtain valid insurance.
   d) None of the above.

ℹ️ Licence plates do not move with vehicles, they move with vehicle owners. All vehicle changes must be reported to a registry agent.

166. **The area that is not visible when looking in your side and rear view mirros is known as?**

   a) Time zone.
   b) Blind spot
   c) Black hole.
   d) Danger area.

ℹ️ Before changing lanes, check your mirrors, check your blind spot by doing a shoulder check, signal, check again and then move into the next lane.

167. **If driving in fog that becomes very dense, what should you do?**

   a) Carefully pass vehicles that are moving too slowly.
   b) Stop on the road and wait for the fog to clear.
   c) Turn on emergency flashers and pull off the road completely into a safe parking area.
   d) Increase the space margin with the vehicle in front of you so that you may follow it safely.

ℹ️ Do not become the first vehicle hit in a chain-reaction collision. Get off the road completely and keep emergency lights flashing. Wait until fog has lifted before driving.

168. What causes a vehicle to hydroplane?

a) Only specialty racing tires can cause hydroplaning.

b) Hydroplaning is caused by ice on the roadway.

c) When a layer of water between the road surface and the tires causes the tires to lose contact with the road. This can result in the vehicle skidding out of control.

d) Hydroplaning can occur if a vehicle is driving at a slow rate of speed.

ⓘ In wet conditions decrease speed, avoid using cruise control and increase space cushions to reduce the risk of hydroplaning.

169. If you skid on a slippery road surface what should you do?

a) Steer your vehicle into the direction you want to go.

b) Steer your vehicle into the opposite direction you want to go.

c) Apply gas to quickly get out of the skid.

d) Turn off the ignition.

ⓘ Skids generally happen because a vehicle is travelling too fast for road, weather, or traffic conditions. In a skid remove your foot from the brake pedal and steer the front of your vehicle into the direction you want to go.

170. What is black ice?

a) When snow is mixed with mud and then freezes.

b) When newly paved roads are wet.

c) When moisture freezes on the road and a thin hard-to-see layer of ice forms.

d) When ice is mixed with snow.

ⓘ Black ice can form anywhere especially on bridges which get extra cold air from below. This causes the temperature to drop more quickly on the bridge forming ice sooner.

171. What are the requirements for the fully licensed driver that accompanies a learner driver?

a) The person must be a fully licensed non-GDL probationary driver.

b) The fully licensed driver must be 18 years of age or older.

c) The fully licensed driver must sit next to the driver in the front seat.

d) All of the above.

ⓘ The fully licensed driver should also not have their ability to take over the wheel impaired by drugs or alcohol.

172. What are you not allowed to do when you have your learner's licence?

a) Drive between midnight and 5:00 a.m.

b) Drive between midnight and 6:00 a.m.

c) Drive between 9:00 p.m. and 5:00 a.m.

d) Drive between 9:00 p.m. and 6:00 a.m.

ⓘ In the learner stage you must adhere to restricted driving times and only drive between 5:00 a.m. and midnight.

173. Which of the following is false about probationary Class 5 licence holders?

a) You must be a probationary driver for at least 2 years.

b) You may have a blood alcohol level of .05 or less.

c) You may have as many passengers as there are seatbelts.

d) You can not accompany a learner driver as their coach.

ⓘ Since the probationary licence lasts at least 24 months, more privileges exist with this class than with a learner's licence. However, alcohol consumption is not one of these.

174. If you refuse to provide a roadside breath sample what can happen?

a) You get a warning that will go on your record and you can not refuse when asked next time.

b) You have 24 hours to show up for a test.

c) You have the option of going to the police station and providing a breath sample there.

d) Your licence is automatically suspended for 3 months.

ⓘ Do not avoid a breath sample by thinking you can "get off" the charges. You will be charged with failing to provide a breath sample and the conviction is the same as for impaired driving, which is a federal offence.

175. Which of these circumstances can give you a suspension or impaired driving charge?

a) If you are in the GDL program and have any alcohol in your blood.

b) If you have a blood alcohol level over .08.

c) If a peace officer deems your driving ability to be affected by drugs or alcohol.

d) All of the above.

ⓘ Impaired driving kills people. Always make other arrangements so you, and others, arrive alive. Take a taxi, public transit, spend the night and sleep it off, call a friend or parent for pick-up or have a designated driver.

176. When driving on a multi-lane highway, what should the far right lane be used for?

a) Slow moving traffic.

b) Fast moving traffic.

c) Emergency vehicles only.

d) Emergency parking.

ⓘ On multi-lane highways slower traffic should drive in the far right lane, allowing faster vehicles to pass in the left lane.

177. Outside of an urban area, what is the maximum speed limit for a primary highway, unless posted otherwise?
a) 60 km/h.
b) 70 km/h.
c) 90 km/h.
d) 100 km/h.

ⓘ Speed limits indicate the maximum speed you are allowed to drive when conditions are good. Slow down when rain, snow, fog or other hazardous conditions occur.

178. What does keeping a space cushion around your vehicle mean?
a) To maintain adequate tire pressure of all tires.
b) To keep enough space between you and the vehicle ahead of you.
c) To keep enough space between your vehicle and any vehicles in front, behind and to your sides allowing you adequate time to see, respond and avoid a potential problem.
d) Refers to airbags.

ⓘ Remember your space cushion will need to be larger when there are conditions that can affect your stopping distance.

179. What should you do if your vehicle breaks down on a busy highway?
a) Move off the road safely.
b) Switch on your hazard lights.
c) Avoid making roadside repairs on a busy highway.
d) All of the above.

ⓘ Avoid stopping in a tunnel or on a bridge. Carry a cell phone whenever you travel in the event of an emergency.

180. **What should you do if you get a flat tire while driving?**
   a) Step on the gas pedal and quickly move off the road.
   b) Firmly steer into the direction you want to go and remove your foot from the gas pedal.
   c) Honk your horn for help.
   d) None of the above.

ⓘ Flat tires can be dangerous. Remain calm, take your foot off the gas pedal and firmly steer where you want to go.

181. **Why should you be cautious when a large vehicle is backing up?**
   a) Large vehicles do not have side mirrors.
   b) The driver of a large vehicle may not be able to see you.
   c) The blind spots on large vehicles are large.
   d) Both b) and c).

ⓘ The blind spots on large vehicles are much larger than the blind spots in automobiles so be extra cautious around large vehicles whether they are backing up or driving on the roadway.

182. **What must you do if in an accident with no personal injuries and damages over $2,000?**
   a) Exchange information with the other party and leave.
   b) Call police and give them as much information as possible about the accident and damages.
   c) Leave the scene as insurance handles this.
   d) All of the above.

ⓘ Remain at the scene and provide help to police about the accident. Exchange required information with other drivers.

183. **What can happen if you are in the GDL program and you have accumulated 8 or more demerit points within a 2-year period?**

    a) Your licence will be suspended for 3 months.

    b) Your licence will be suspended for 1 month.

    c) Your licence will be suspended for 15 days.

    d) You will receive a warning letter in the mail to improve your driving.

ⓘ Carefully review suspension notices which are sent to your address by certified or registered mail. Surrender your licence by the date indicated to a registry agent. Obey all conditions of your suspension.

184. **Which statement about alcohol and its affect on you is true?**

    a) If you eat well and are full, alcohol will not affect you.

    b) You can have more beer because it is not as strong as other alcoholic drinks.

    c) Alcohol combined with other drugs can cause a dangerous reaction.

    d) If you have been driving for years, you will know how to handle a vehicle after a few drinks.

ⓘ Combining 2 alcoholic drinks with just one dose of marijuana can make you as drunk and incoherent as if you had 5 alcoholic drinks. Do not drink or take drugs and drive.

185. **When and how often do you have to renew your driver's licence?**

    a) Every 5 years when you receive a renewal notice in the mail.

    b) You do not have to renew as you have already passed all required tests.

    c) Every 10 years.

    d) Every 20 years.

ⓘ If you do not receive a renewal notice in the mail you are still responsible for ensuring you have a valid driver's licence.

186. What should you remember about cyclists?
- a) Cyclists are considered to be a vehicle unless they are walking their bicycle.
- b) Cyclists have their own set of rules.
- c) You should pass a cyclist as you would any vehicle.
- d) Both a) and c).

ⓘ Cyclists are considered to be a vehicle and should be passed like any vehicle. It is a good practice to allow extra room when passing.

187. In an urban area, is it legal for a driver to back into an intersection or crosswalk?
- a) It is illegal to back into an intersection in an urban area.
- b) It is legal to back into an intersection in an urban area.
- c) It is legal to back into an intersection or a crosswalk provided their aren't any pedestrians.
- d) It is illegal to back into an intersection only during certain hours.

ⓘ Leave enough of a space cushion behind the vehicle in front of you to enable you to safely pull out and pass the vehicle in the event that vehicle stalls.

188. As an Alberta driver what insurance responsibilities do you have?
- a) You are only required to have a valid operator's licence.
- b) You are only required to have current licence plates on the vehicle you are driving.
- c) You must have an operator's licence, vehicle plates, registration and proper insurance.
- d) None of the above.

ⓘ You must have insurance to drive a vehicle. Coverage can only be obtained with a valid licence and current vehicle plates and registration. Plans vary, but the minimum amount of liability insurance must be acquired.

189. What changes must you tell a registry agent about?
a) If your name has changed.
b) If your address has changed.
c) If your licence was lost, stolen or damaged.
d) All of the above.

ⓘ You must keep your licence up-to-date; any change of name, address, or other information needs to be reported to a registry agent within 14 days.

190. Which of these statements is false?
a) You must always have your operator's licence with you while driving a motor vehicle.
b) You must always have the correct licence class with you while driving a motor vehicle.
c) You may use your suspended operator's licence to drive a motor vehicle.
d) You must by law have the minimum amount of motor vehicle insurance to drive in Alberta.

ⓘ There are licence laws that all drivers must follow. It is illegal to drive without a valid licence for the class you are in. Also, you must never drive while under suspension.

191. What should you do if a large animal is in front of you on the road and you can't stop in time?
a) Slow down and if you can see far enough ahead and it is safe to do so steer around the animal.
b) Increase speed and hit the animal to ensure it does not charge you or your passengers.
c) Both of the above.
d) None of the above.

ⓘ Encountering large animals in your path while driving is very dangerous. If the situation does not allow you to steer away from it and you must hit it, do so on an angle while firmly braking and then easing off the brake pedal.

192. Why must you pay special attention while driving in a "weave zone"?

    a) The road curves a lot so you need to pay extra attention in these zones.

    b) The road curves for more than 5 km so you need to pay extra attention while driving in these zones.

    c) Vehicles may be slowing down to exit the highway while others may be speeding up to enter.

    d) Vehicles may be speeding up to exit the highway while others may be slowing down to enter.

ⓘ Be alert and use extra caution in weave zones. Use proper speed and exercise good judgment for space.

193. What are parking lanes on highways intended for?

    a) Parking by any type of vehicle in any circumstance.

    b) For emergency parking only.

    c) A passing lane for any type of vehicle.

    d) None of the above.

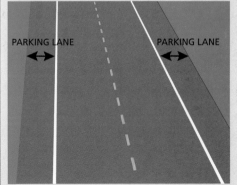

PARKING LANE   PARKING LANE

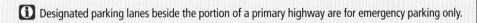

ⓘ Designated parking lanes beside the portion of a primary highway are for emergency parking only.

194. What is the maximum allowed speed in a playground zone?
    a) Unless posted otherwise, 30 km/h from 8:30 am to one hour after sunset every day.
    b) Unless posted otherwise, 35 km/h from 8:30 am to one hour after sunset every day.
    c) The speed for playground zones is 30 km/h, only on weekends.
    d) Unless posted otherwise, 30 km/h from one hour before sunrise to 8:30 pm every day.

ⓘ You may not pass another vehicle travelling in the same direction in a playground zone.

195. When parking downhill beside a curb what should you do?
    a) Make your tires as straight as possible to be parallel with the curb.
    b) The direction of your tires does not matter as long as you set your parking brake.
    c) Turn your tires to the right, move forward slightly so the front right tire touches the curb.
    d) Turn your tires to the left, move forward slightly so the front right tire touches the curb.

ⓘ It is a good practice to always set your parking brake when your vehicle is parked regardless of terrain.

196. What speed limit must you travel when passing stopped emergency vehicles with lights flashing?
    a) You must slow down to 30 km/h, or less if a lower speed limit is indicated.
    b) You must slow down to 60 km/h, or less if a lower speed limit is indicated.
    c) You must slow down to 80 km/h, or less if a lower speed limit is indicated.
    d) You must slow down to 100 km/h, or less if a lower speed limit is indicated.

ⓘ Fines are doubled if you exceed 60 km/h (less if posted) in the lane immediately beside an emergency vehicle.

197. What should you do when following a motorcycle?

a) Allow extra space between your vehicle and the motorcycle as motorcycles are exempt from certain rules of the road.

b) Allow extra space between your vehicle and the motorcycle as motorcycles can stop quickly.

c) Honk your horn to notify them of your presence.

d) Flash your head lights on and off to notify them of your presence.

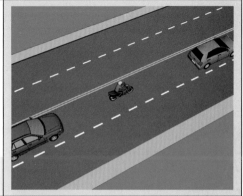

ⓘ When you are following a motorcycle, allow extra space and even more in wet conditions.

198. What does the law state about parking and distance from a curb?

a) You may not park a vehicle more than 50 cm away from a curb.

b) You may not park a vehicle more than 30 cm away from a curb.

c) You may not park a vehicle more than 10 cm away from a curb.

d) You may not park a vehicle more than 2 cm away from a curb.

ⓘ Ensure you do not park so that your wheels are more than 50 cm away from the curb.

199. **When stopped at an intersection how much of a space cushion should you leave between you and the vehicle in front?**

    a) 10 car lengths.

    b) 5 car lengths.

    c) Enough space so that you can pull out, if required, without having to back up.

    d) Enough space so that you can pull out, if required, by only backing up slightly.

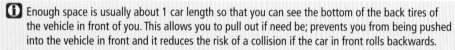

ⓘ Enough space is usually about 1 car length so that you can see the bottom of the back tires of the vehicle in front of you. This allows you to pull out if need be; prevents you from being pushed into the vehicle in front and it reduces the risk of a collision if the car in front rolls backwards.

200. **What is the best way to handle "off-road recovery"?**

    a) Hold both hands firmly to the steering wheel, press on the brakes firmly, check for traffic and return to the road.

    b) Hold both hands firmly to the steering wheel, ease off the gas pedal, check for traffic and return to the road.

    c) Hold both hands firmly to the steering wheel, ease off the gas pedal, return to the road quickly.

    d) None of the above.

ⓘ If you find yourself off the main portion of the roadway, avoid braking suddenly. Instead, ease off the gas pedal while firmly holding the steering wheel. Do proper traffic checks and return to the main road.

The Road Test

After you have been driving the appropriate length of time and gained the proper skills and experience to be a safe and responsible driver, you may book a road test. You can book a Class 5 road test after 12 months. Your driving experience should have included adequate practice time before your first road test. After 24

months of driving as a GDL probationary Class 5 driver, of which the last 12 months have been suspension free, you may book

an advanced road test. At least 60 hours of driving experience is recommended before taking an advanced road test.

Both road tests may assess similar skills, with the advanced road test requiring a higher level of skills and knowledge. During the advanced road test you may be asked questions about road hazards and how to identify other driving related challenges.

Arrive on time and well ahead of your scheduled road test appointment. Bring a vehicle in good working order. Also bring your driver's licence, vehicle registration and insurance documents, permit for the test, enough gas for at least an hour of driving and glasses if you need to wear them for driving.

Note: You may not drive with an expired licence. Your learner's licence will expire. If you have not booked and passed a road test or have enough driving experience by then you will have to renew it. Depending on how long your learner licence has been expired, fees and requirements to reinstate it may vary. Find out more from a registry agent office.

Before the examiner asks you to do a specific driving task he or she will ask you to perform some inside vehicle checks, such as sounding the horn and checking brake lights, turn signals and steering. You will also be asked to use and describe two interior controls, such as the rear-view mirror or parking brake, for example. Are you comfortable and will you be safe? Have you adjusted mirrors, seats, head restraints etc.? The examiner will provide you with route information so you know where you will be heading. Then they will observe how you control your vehicle and how well you drive.

The examiner will also be checking how well you observe everything around you: using your mirrors, checking blind spots and making eye contact with pedestrians and other drivers. You will also be graded on how well you react to traffic lights, road signs, pavement markings, speed limits, hazards and traffic.

The following pages contain detailed instruction on how to perform certain manoeuvres on road tests. This is not an inclusive list. Study what you have obtained from any driving course you have taken as well as all sources to help you prepare for your applicable driving test.

The Class 5 Road Test will include:

✔ Left and right turns

✔ Managing controlled and uncontrolled intersections

✔ Speed limits

✔ Changing lanes

✔ Driving in school or playground sections noting times and speed

✔ Parallel parking

✔ Hill parking

✔ Vehicle controls and how you use them

The Advanced Road Test will include:

✔ Many left and right turns

✔ Varying speed limits

✔ Stopping and driving through controlled and uncontrolled intersections

✔ Approaching and stopping at crosswalks

✔ Approaching and stopping at controlled and uncontrolled railroad crossings

✔ Changing lanes

✔ Handling curves

✔ Emergency and hazard exercises

✔ Highway driving—entering and exiting

✔ Driving in traffic

✔ Driving in school or playground sections

✔ Various parking methods

Left and Right Turns

Approaching a Turn

1. Traffic check

Look around you. Use your mirrors, and if changing lanes check your blind spot.

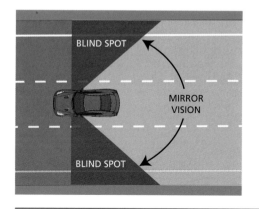

2. Signal and use correct lane

Turn on the appropriate signal at about 1/3 of a block or 30 metres from the intersection in urban areas (100 m in rural areas) and slow down. If there are vehicles on the side roads or driveways before your turn, wait until you have passed these vehicles before you signal so those drivers will not think you are turning before the intersection. Move into the far left or far right lane when it is safe to do so.

3. Speed and traffic check

Gradually slow down as you come to the intersection and be aware of all signs before you turn. If you have a manual transmission, you can downshift into a lower gear as you reduce speed. Do not coast with your foot on the clutch. Check for other road users, such as pedestrians and bicyclists, by doing shoulder checks. Be sure to yield to pedestrians.

4. Space and wheels

Maintain a distance of 2 to 3 seconds behind the vehicle ahead of you while slowing down. If turning right ensure you are at least 1 m from the curb. If turning left keep your wheels straight.

Stopping Before a Turn (if required due to traffic, a stop sign, or a red light)

1. Stop

Before you slow down, take a look at everything around you. Check traffic behind you by looking into all mirrors. Look well enough ahead and keep your chin level and not tilted up. If your chin is up it will force your eyes to look down causing you to brake late and too hard.

Make a complete stop and wait for traffic and/or lights to clear. When safe, move forward to start your turn. If you have to stop after passing the stop line and are in the intersection, do not back up.

2. Space

If a vehicle is ahead of you at an intersection, ensure you have enough space to pass the vehicle without backing up. This cushion of space lets you pull out if the vehicle stalls; it reduces risk of collision if the vehicle rolls backward; and it minimizes or avoids a collision if you are hit from behind.

3. Stop line

If there are no vehicles ahead of you as you approach an intersection with a red light or stop sign, stop behind the marked stop line. If there is no marked stop line, stop at the crosswalk whether it is marked or not.

If there is no crosswalk, stop at the edge of the sidewalk. And if there is no sidewalk, stop at the edge of the intersection.

4. Wheels

Keep your wheels straight if you are turning left.

Make sure your wheels are straight as you wait to make your left turn. This ensures that your vehicle will not get pushed into oncoming traffic. When waiting to make a right turn, also keep your wheels straight

so that you will not hit pedestrians if you get hit from behind. At large intersections with curved sidewalk curbs when turning right angle your vehicle so that no other car can fit between you and the curb.

The Actual Turn

1. Traffic check

Before pulling into the intersection, look left, ahead, and right to make sure that the way is clear. If you are unsure about who has the right-of-way, try to make eye contact with the drivers or pedestrians in question. Check your blind spot before turning in case it is possible for another vehicle to overtake you. If a pedestrian or another vehicle with the right-of-way has to get out of your way then, you have not checked traffic properly.

2. Hands

Your risk of collision is greatest when turning so to maintain control of your vehicle keep both hands on the steering wheel throughout the turn.

3. Gears

If you are driving a vehicle with manual transmission, if necessary, shift gears after the vehicle starts moving but before the turn.

4. Speed

Start moving once you have ensured it is safe. Drive slowly enough to maintain control of your vehicle and increase speed as you complete the turn.

5. Entering new lane

Once you have cleared the intersection, enter your corresponding lane without going over lane markings or curbs.

Completing the Turn

1. Lane

Enter the lane that you turned from. When turning left onto a multi-lane road, turn into the left lane. Return to normal speed and move into the curb lane when it is safe to do so. When turning right, move into the right lane; if it is blocked with parked vehicles, move over to the next available lane.

2. Traffic check

Check your mirrors as you return to normal speed and make yourself fully aware of the traffic on this new street. Many conditions may have changed from the street you turned from.

3. Speed

Return to normal traffic speed but adapt and blend in with the traffic of the new road. Remember not to exceed the speed limit.

Stopping at Intersections

The Approach

1. Traffic check

Before you slow down, take a look at everything around you. Check traffic behind you by looking into all mirrors. Look well enough ahead and keep your chin level. If your chin is tilted up it will

force your eyes to look down causing you to brake late and too hard.

2. Speed

As you near the intersection, gradually reduce speed. If you have a manual transmission, downshift into a lower gear as you reduce speed. Do not coast by keeping your foot on the clutch.

3. Space

Stay at least 2 to 3 seconds behind the vehicle ahead of you.

The Stop

1. Stop

Cover the brake pedal with your foot and stop gradually to avoid braking late, which can cause someone to hit you from behind. Make a complete stop without rolling forward or backward. When traffic allows, move forward to ensure the way is clear and start moving across the intersection. If you need to stop after passing the stop line and are in the intersection, do not back up.

2. Space and wheels

If a vehicle is ahead of you at an intersection, ensure you have enough space to pass the vehicle without backing up. This cushion of space lets you pull out if the vehicle stalls; it reduces the risk of a collision if the vehicle rolls backward; and it minimizes or avoids a front-end collision if you are hit from behind.

3. Stop line

If there are no vehicles ahead of you as you approach an intersection with a red light or stop sign, stop behind the marked stop line. If there is no marked stop line, stop at the crosswalk whether it is marked or not. If there is no crosswalk, stop at the edge of the sidewalk. If there is no sidewalk, stop at the edge of the intersection. Remember to keep your wheels straight.

Driving Through

1. Traffic check

Before entering an intersection, look left, ahead, and right to make sure nothing is in your path. Do not enter the intersection if traffic is backed up on the other side.

If you are unsure about who has the right-of-way, try to make eye contact with the drivers or pedestrians in question. If a pedestrian or another vehicle with the right-of-way has to get out of your way, then you have not checked traffic properly.

2. Hands

Your risk of collision is greatest when crossing the intersection so to maintain control of your vehicle keep both hands on the steering wheel.

3. Gears

If you are driving a vehicle with manual transmission, maintain more control by not changing gears while crossing. If necessary, shift gears after the vehicle starts moving but before it is too far into the intersection.

4. Traffic check

After going through the intersection, check your mirrors as you return to normal speed and make yourself fully aware of all traffic.

5. Speed

Start moving once you have ensured it is safe. Return to normal traffic speed but adapt and blend in with traffic. Remember not to exceed the speed limit.

Driving Through Intersections

The Approach

1. Traffic check

As you near the intersection, look ahead, left and right to see if there is any traffic on the intersecting road. If it is necessary to slow down, take your foot off the gas pedal and check on the traffic situation in your rear-view mirror.

2. Speed

Maintain your speed when proceeding through the intersection unless you see that traffic may cross your path. If that is the case, reduce speed or hold your foot over the brake pedal so you are prepared to stop if necessary. Be extra alert for pedestrians and vehicles coming into the intersection, as well as vehicles approaching at higher speeds.

3. Space

Maintain a distance of 2 to 3 seconds behind the vehicle ahead of you.

Driving Through

1. Lane

Stay within your lane. Do not change lanes or drive across lane markings in the intersection. Slow down or stop if your lane is blocked by a left-turning vehicle or a vehicle turning into the intersection from the right.

2. Speed

Assume regular speed by keeping your foot on the gas pedal, ensuring you do not exceed the speed limit.

3. Hands

Your risk of collision is greatest when crossing the intersection so to maintain control of your vehicle keep both hands on the steering wheel.

4. Gears

If you are driving a vehicle with manual transmission, maintain more control when crossing the intersection by not changing gears. If necessary, shift gears after the vehicle is moving but before it is in the intersection. The less gear shifting, the more vehicle control.

5. Traffic check

If you had to slow down at the intersection, check your mirrors before resuming normal traffic speed.

Stopping at Crosswalks

The Approach

1. Traffic check

Scan the roadway and look at everything around you by looking into all mirrors. Be aware of pedestrian or school crosswalk signs. Sometimes these may have flashing amber lights. Look well enough

ahead and keep your chin level. If your chin is tilted up it will force your eyes to look down causing you to brake late and too hard.

2. Speed

As you near the crosswalk, gradually reduce speed. Crosswalk signs with flashing amber lights mean you must reduce your speed limit to 30 km/h or less unless a sign indicates otherwise. If you have a manual transmission, downshift into a lower gear as you reduce speed.

3. Space

Stay at least 2 to 3 seconds behind the vehicle ahead of you.

4. Lane

Never change lanes or pass another vehicle while approaching a crosswalk. This could obstruct someone's view and they may not see a pedestrian crossing.

The Stop

1. Stop

If a pedestrian has shown their intention to cross, whether the crosswalk is marked or not you must bring your vehicle to a complete stop and yield the right-of-way to the crossing pedestrian. Be aware that not all crosswalks are marked but most intersections have crosswalks.

2. Stop Line

You must stop far enough back so other vehicles in any direction can stop in time for the pedestrian. If there is no marked stop line, stop at the crosswalk whether it is marked or not. Wait until the pedestrian has completely crossed and is off the road before driving forward.

Driving Through

1. Traffic check

Check all mirrors and check to ensure pedestrians have crossed the road safely before moving forward. Remember, some people may take more time to cross.

2. Speed

Gradually accelerate to the speed of traffic, without exceeding the speed limit.

Stopping at Railway Crossings

The Approach

1. Traffic check

Scan the roadway and look well ahead to observe all possible railway crossing signs and road markings. Some signs provide advance warning of approaching tracks. There may also be pavement markings with an "X" indicating you are approaching a railway crossing. Some signs will have a stop sign and flashing signal lights as well as gates.

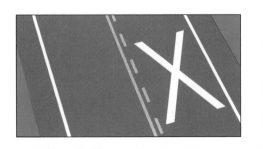

2. Speed

As you near the tracks reduce speed and obey posted speed limits, which are sometimes considerably reduced. While slowing down listen carefully for warning bells.

3. Space

Stay at least 2 to 3 seconds behind the vehicle ahead of you. Be prepared to stop for commercial vehicles, such as trucks and company vans, which may need to stop at all railway crossings due to company policy, regardless of signs.

The Stop

1. Stop and stop line

Whenever you hear warning bells or see a train within 500 m of a railway crossing you must stop. Some railway crossings have stop signs so you must bring your vehicle to a complete stop between 5–15 m from the nearest rail. Flashing signal lights and ringing bells also indicate an approaching train requiring you to stop 5 m back from the nearest rail. There are also railway crossings with gates, bells and flashing red lights. You must stop when lights flash and bells ring, which will be before gates are lowered.

If traffic is present don't get trapped on railway tracks. When approaching in this circumstance, stop your vehicle before the tracks; if no signals require you to stop proceed only if you can fully cross the tracks. When in doubt always slow down and stop; avoid a deadly collision between you and a train.

Driving Through

1. Traffic check

Check all indicators. Do not proceed until trains have passed *and* signal lights have stopped flashing, bells have stopped ringing and gates have been raised. Double check your right and left side in case a second train comes on another track from a different direction. Trains take a long time to stop—a kilometre or more—so do not proceed until safe.

2. Gears

If you are driving a vehicle with manual transmission, for best control of your vehicle do not change gears when crossing railway tracks.

3. Speed

If you had to stop, proceed slowly and gradually resume the speed of traffic without exceeding the speed limit. Drive straight and do not make any turns, including U-turns, near a railway crossing.

Changing Lanes

1. Traffic check

First, make a visual sweep of everything around you. Look ahead, in the mirrors, and check your blind spot. If you are on a multi-lane highway, make sure another vehicle in the far lane is not moving into the same lane you are.

2. Signal

When there is enough room for you to change lanes, put your signal on. Check your blind spot with a shoulder check once more before moving into the other lane. Your signal alerts drivers behind you as to what you want to do. Even if there does not appear to be enough room due

to traffic to make a lane change, with your signal on, traffic behind you will know your intentions.

3. Space

Make sure you have a 2 to 3 second distance behind the vehicle ahead of you. If there is another lane beside the one you are moving into, take care not to move into the blind spot of another vehicle.

4. Speed

Adjust your speed so that you are moving at the pace of traffic in the new lane without exceeding the speed limit.

5. Change

Gradually and smoothly move into the centre of the new lane.

6. Hands

Keep both hands on the steering wheel for best control.

7. Turn off signal

Once you have changed lanes, turn off your signal.

Curves

1. Speed

Before embarking on a curve, it helps to determine a safe speed. To do this look for signs that display the speed, determine how sharp the curve is, and consider the type of road surface you are driving on. The safe speed should be achieved by the time you are approximately 30 m into the curve. If you can not see all the way around the curve, slow down. The curve may be tighter than you think or oncoming traffic could be approaching.

Make sure you slow down before the curve to avoid braking in it. Once in the curve, maintain a slow steady speed. As you approach the end of the curve, accelerate to normal speed. Vehicles with manual transmissions should not shift gears in the curve. This will provide more control and reduce the the chance of the wheels losing contact with the road surface while downshifting.

2. Lane

Once you have entered the curve, look as far as you can around it. This will help you drive in a smooth line while staying in the centre of the lane. Looking only at the road right ahead of you makes you likely to veer across the lane causing you to constantly steer to correct your driving. If you are in a right-hand curve, for example, steer your vehicle slightly to the right ensuring you do not over steer.

3. Speed

Once you are halfway into the curve, accelerate to normal speed, if conditions permit you to do so.

The Highway

Entering

1. Traffic check

When driving on a highway entrance ramp, as soon as you see highway traffic approaching behind you, check your mirrors and blind spot to find a safe place to merge. Make sure you are a safe distance behind vehicles in front. Keep checking your mirrors, your blind spot, and the vehicle ahead of you until you can merge safely.

2. Signal

Turn your signal on as soon as highway traffic can see your vehicle on the ramp.

3. Space

While merging with highway traffic, stay at least 2 to 3 seconds behind the vehicle ahead of you. Do not merge right beside another vehicle or into someone's blind spot. Sometimes traffic moves at such high speed that it is hard to maintain an ideal following distance. Adjust speed accordingly and keep inside the lane markings.

4. Speed

Merging on the highway is a combination of slowing down and speeding up. Prior to the merge, you will enter via a curving entrance ramp. Use a speed that is not too fast for the curve. Then, once in the straight acceleration lane, speed up to match the flow of highway traffic. Control speed to merge smoothly.

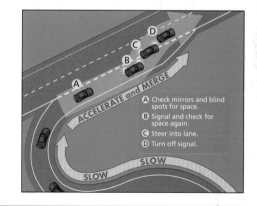

ACCELERATE and MERGE

Ⓐ Check mirrors and blind spots for space.
Ⓑ Signal and check for space again.
Ⓒ Steer into lane.
Ⓓ Turn off signal.

SLOW SLOW SLOW

5. Merge

Ensure you have passed the solid white line and then merge smoothly with highway traffic to the centre of the nearest highway lane.

6. Turn off signal

Once you have merged, turn off your signal.

Driving Along

1. Traffic check

While driving in the same lane, keep a constant check on the traffic around you. Check your mirrors often.

2. Speed

Maintain a steady speed. Exceeding the speed limit is to be avoided, as is driving too slowly. Ensure you can see where you will be 12 to 15 seconds ahead in case dangerous situations or obstacles lie ahead.

3. Space

Keep at least a 2 to 3 second distance behind the vehicle ahead of you. Make this distance even bigger or change lanes if another vehicle is following you too closely. Large vehicles can block your view so do not drive behind them. Try to maintain space on all sides of your vehicle. Avoid driving in the blind spots of other vehicles and never drive in the highway parking lane.

Exiting

1. Traffic check

Do a complete traffic check before moving into the deceleration lane. If there is a right lane beside you, check your blind spot by doing a shoulder check.

2. Signal

Turn your signal on before reaching the deceleration lane.

3. Deceleration lane

Using smooth movement and staying inside the lane markings, begin to enter the deceleration lane. Do not cross solid lines if there is more than one deceleration lane.

4. Speed

Wait until you are completely in the deceleration lane before slowing down. Once in the deceleration lane and exit ramp, gradually decrease speed ensuring you do not go too fast on the curve. Vehicles with manual transmissions should downshift while reducing speed.

5. Space

Maintain a 2 to 3 second distance behind the vehicle ahead of you.

6. Turn signal off

Once on the exit ramp, turn off your signal.

Driving in Traffic or Business Sections

1. Traffic check

Business areas are much more cluttered than other roads. Vehicles and pedestrians can enter the road from a number of areas. There are more pedestrian crossings as well as entrances to businesses, institutions and parking lots. Railway crossings and bicycles may also be part of a business section. Look left and right at all entrances to check for vehicles or pedestrians.

2. Mirror check

Check your mirrors often while driving. If traffic is heavy or if vehicles are travelling at different speeds, check mirrors more frequently.

3. Lane

Drive in the safest lane (usually the curb lane). If the curb lane is blocked with parked cars or traffic, drive in the centre lane. Stay in the middle of your lane. See where you will be in the next 12 to 15 seconds by looking ahead and changing lanes if you need to avoid any obstacles ahead.

4. Speed

Drive at a steady speed. Avoid driving too slowly or exceeding the speed limit. See where you will be in the next 12 to

15 seconds by looking ahead and changing speed if you need to avoid any obstacles ahead.

5. Space

Keep a minimum 2 to 3 second distance behind you and from the vehicle ahead of you. Make this distance even bigger if you are being followed too closely. Try to maintain space on all sides of your vehicle, especially on multi-lane roads, and avoid driving in the blind spots of other vehicles. In slow traffic, large vehicles may block your view of what is ahead so avoid driving behind them. When you stop behind another vehicle, allow enough space to see its rear wheels so that you can pull around it without having to back up.

Driving in School or Playground Sections

1. Traffic check

Especially on residential streets, be aware of school and playground areas. Constantly scan the street and be on the lookout for school zone and playground zone signs. Slow down and be extra cautious in these areas. Also be alert for small children who may run out into the street from playgrounds or who may be playing on or near curbs. Be on the look-out for children's toys and bikes indicating children are nearby.

2. Mirror check

Check mirrors often while driving. Knowing what is happening around you in front, behind and on all sides is the best way to react to situations.

3. Lane

Stay in the centre of the lane. Some streets will not have lane markings, in which case you should stay in the centre of the travelled part of the road away from children, pedestrians and parked vehicles. If you are approaching a hill or curve where you are unable to see ahead on the road, slow down immediately. Never change lanes or pass another vehicle travelling in the same direction in a school or playground zone if zone days and hours are in effect.

4. Speed

The speed limit is 30 km/h in both urban and rural school zones. Drive this speed during school days during these hours: 8:00 am.–9:30 a.m., 11:30 a.m.–1:30 p.m. and 3:00 p.m.–4:30 p.m. unless a sign provides other speed, day and time information. The speed limit is also 30 km/h in both urban and rural playground zones unless a sign indicates otherwise. This speed limit is in effect in playground zones every day from 8:30 a.m. to 1 hour after sunset.

5. End of zone speed

School and playground zones end when a higher speed is posted or if a sign tells you the zone has ended. Before increasing speed to the posted speed limit do a scan of the street to ensure no children are present or nearby. Then gradually increase to the posted speed limit.

END SCHOOL ZONE

Parallel Parking

The Approach

1. Traffic check

Check your mirrors before slowing down. Check your blind spot before getting into position to back up.

2. Signal

Before slowing down, turn on your signal. If there are vehicles on side roads or driveways between you and where you plan to stop, wait until you have passed them so those drivers will not think you are turning before your parking position.

3. Speed

Gradually slow down. If you have a manual transmission, reduce speed while you downshift into a lower gear.

4. Stop

Tap your brakes a few times to warn vehicles behind you that you are planning to stop. Stop parallel to the parked vehicle in front of the empty parking space. This is when your rear bumper is inline with their rear bumper or, if no vehicle is there, stop where it would be. Allow 1 m of space between your vehicle and the parked vehicle. Stop when you are completely in front of the empty parking space.

Parking

1. Traffic check

Before you put your vehicle in reverse, check your mirrors and both blind spots to ensure that nothing is in your way.

2. Back up

Begin to back up into the empty space while turning the steering wheel to the right sharply. As you turn, the front of your car will swing out so ensure you have enough space and the way is clear. Your vehicle should be at approximately a 45-degree angle to the curb at this point. Stop and do another traffic check. When safe, continue to reverse slowly. When you are about halfway in, straighten your wheels while continuing to back up.

When you have passed the car in front of you steer to the left while continuing to slowly back up inline with the curb.

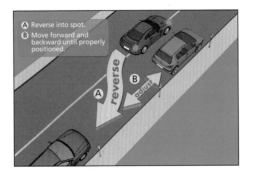

3. Stop

Once in the space, move your vehicle forward and/or backward until it fits within the pavement markings. Ensure you are not more than 50 cm from the curb, and then stop. Whether there are pavement markings or not, make sure you allow enough room for vehicles in front and behind you to get out of their parking space. While parking never hit the curb or bump other vehicles. If there is no curb, park on the untravelled part of the road.

4. Park

Shift your vehicle into park and set the parking brake. If you have a manual transmission, shift into low or reverse, turn off the engine and set the parking brake. Position wheels in the correct direction to ensure your vehicle does not roll into the roadway.

Resume Driving

1. Start

Turn your engine on and release the parking brake. If required back up as close to the vehicle behind you without hitting it. This will provide you with enough space to exit your parking spot. Shift into the appropriate gear to get back on the road.

2. Signal

Turn on your left signal light.

3. Traffic check

Check your mirrors and blind spot before pulling out of the parking space.

4. Speed

Accelerate smoothly as you return to normal traffic speed but adapt and blend

in with traffic. Remember to not exceed the speed limit.

5. Turn off signal

Once back on the road, turn your signal off.

Hill Parking—Uphill With a Curb

The Approach

1. Traffic check

Get into the correct lane by checking your mirrors, ensuring the way is clear from all sides.

2. Signal

Before slowing down, turn on your signal so those in front or behind you know of your intention to park.

3. Speed

Decelerate. When at a very slow speed move to the right side of the curb and stop.

Move forward to adjust your vehicle position if it is more than 50 cm from the curb.

Parking

1. Traffic check

Do a traffic check on your left side and then when safe move forward.

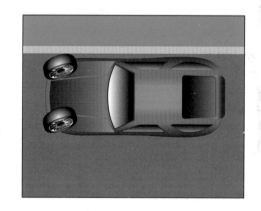

2. Move forward

Slowly move forward while sharply turning the steering wheel a full left turn.

3. Reverse gear

Do a traffic check before reversing slowly and allow your vehicle to gradually move backward until the front right tire touches the curb slightly.

4. Neutral gear

Shift your vehicle into neutral to allow it to rest back against the curb.

5. Park and brake

Shift into park and apply the parking brake.

Resume Driving

1. Start

Turn your engine on and keep your foot firmly on the brake pedal. Shift into forward gear.

2. Traffic check

Check your mirrors and blind spot with a shoulder check; when safe, release the parking brake.

3. Signal

With your foot on the brake pedal, put your left signal on.

4. Parking brake

Do another traffic check in all mirrors and a shoulder check before driving away from the curb.

5. Speed

Slowly move away from the curb and enter the nearest traffic lane when it is safe to do so.

6. Turn off signal

Once back on the road, turn your signal off.

Hill Parking—Uphill Without a Curb

The Approach

1. Traffic check

Get into the correct lane by checking your mirrors, ensuring the way is clear from all sides.

2. Signal

Before slowing down, turn on your signal so those in front or behind you know of your intention to park.

3. Speed

Decelerate. When at a very slow speed move to the right side of the road and stop parallel to it. Move forward to adjust your vehicle position if necessary.

Parking

1. Traffic check

Do a traffic check on the front right side. When safe move forward.

2. Move forward

Slowly move forward while sharply turning the steering wheel to the right, without going off the travelled part of the roadway. Then stop.

3. Park and brake

Keep foot firmly on the brake pedal, shift into park, set parking brake.

Resume Driving

1. Start

Turn your engine on and keep your foot firmly on the brake pedal. Shift into reverse or neutral gear.

2. Traffic check

Check your mirrors and blind spot with a shoulder check; when safe, release the parking brake.

3. Reverse gear

For a short distance, slowly move backward and steer sharply to the left until front wheels are positioned straight. Then stop.

4. Forward gear

Keep your foot firmly on the brake pedal, shift into forward gear.

5. Signal

Do another traffic check in all mirrors and a shoulder check and then put your left signal on.

6. Speed

Slowly move away from the roadway edge and enter the nearest traffic lane when it is safe to do so.

7. Turn off signal

Once back on the road, turn your signal off.

Downhill Parking—With or Without a Curb

The Approach

1. Traffic check

Get into the correct lane by checking your mirrors,

ensuring the way is clear from all sides.

2. Signal

Before slowing down, turn on your signal so those in front or behind you know of your intention to park.

3. Speed

Decelerate. When at a very slow speed move to the right side of the road and stop parallel to it or to the curb if there is one. Move forward to adjust your vehicle position if necessary.

Parking

1. Traffic check

Do a traffic check on your left side and then when safe move forward.

2. Move forward

Slowly move forward while turning the steering wheel a half-turn to the left. Then sharply steer right for a full turn as the vehicle is moving forward slowly. While slowly moving allow the front right tire to slightly touch the curb.

3. With a curb

If parking downhill with a curb, shift into neutral and release your foot from the brake pedal allowing your vehicle to position itself against the curb.

4. Park and brake

Place foot firmly on the brake pedal, shift into park, set the parking brake.

Resume Driving

1. Start

Turn your engine on and keep your foot firmly on the brake pedal. Shift into reverse or neutral gear.

2. Traffic check

Check your mirrors, and your blind spot with a shoulder check; when safe, release the parking brake.

3. Reverse Gear

For a short distance, slowly move backward and steer sharply to the left until front wheels are straight. Then stop.

4. Forward gear

Keep your foot firmly on the brake pedal and shift into forward gear.

5. Signal

Do another traffic check in all mirrors and a shoulder check and then put your left signal on.

6. Speed

Slowly move away from the roadway edge and enter the nearest traffic lane when it is safe to do so.

7. Turn off signal

Once back on the road, turn your signal off.

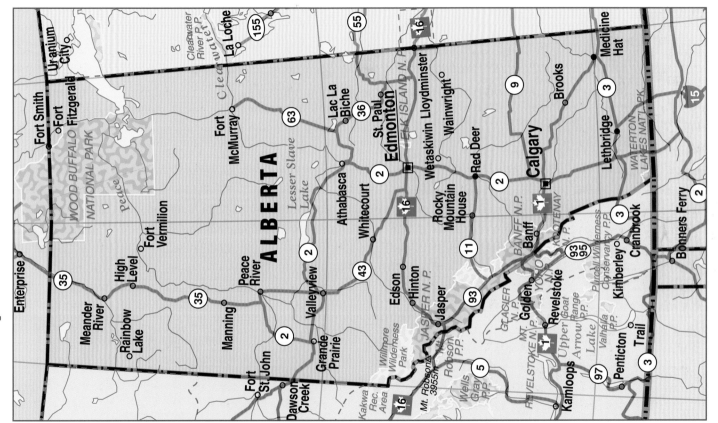

Customer Response Card

Thank you for purchasing this Driver's Study Guide!

Our goal is to provide you with the information you need to pass Alberta driving tests.

Please complete the information below so we will be able to serve you and others better in the future. We value your comments and suggestions for improvements. Let us know what you think. Comments can also be e-mailed to: feedback@cccmaps.com.

(This information is for internal use ONLY and will NOT be distributed or sold to any external third party.)

Your Name: _____

Address: _____

City: _____ Postal Code: _____

Phone Number: _____ E-mail:_____

1. Age Group:

[ ] 14–24   [ ] 25–31   [ ] 32–40   [ ] 41–50   [ ] 51–70   [ ] 71–81   [ ] 82+

2. Where did you purchase your Driver's Study Guide? (store name & location) _____

_____

3. What did you like best about the Driver's Study Guide?_____

_____

4. What did you like least about it? _____

_____

5. What would you add/change in the Driver's Study Guide?_____

_____

6. Did you pass your applicable test after reading the Driver's Study Guide?

[ ] YES   [ ] NO

7. Why do you think you passed or failed?_____

_____

8. Please provide any additional comments or suggestions you have: _____

_____

Fax toll free or mail to:

Canadian Cartographics Corporation
70 Bloor Street East
Oshawa, Ontario
L1H 3M2

Fax: 905.723.6677

r.6